Meditations

Forty Dhamma Talks

Thanissaro Bhikkhu
(Geoffrey DeGraff)

for free distribution

Contents

Contents

Introduction

The daily schedule at Metta Forest Monastery includes a group interview in the late afternoon, and a chanting session followed by a group meditation period later in the evening. The Dhamma talks included in this volume were given during the evening meditation sessions, and in many cases covered issues raised at the interviews—either in the questions asked or lurking behind the questions. Often these issues touched on a variety of topics on a variety of different levels in the practice. This explains the range of topics covered in individual talks.

I have edited the talks with an eye to making them readable while at the same time trying to preserve some of the flavor of the spoken word. In a few instances I have added passages or rearranged the material to make the treatment of specific topics more coherent and complete, but for the most part I have kept the editing to a minimum. Don't expect polished essays.

The people listening to these talks were familiar with the meditaiton instructions included in "Method 2" in *Keeping the Breath in Mind* by Ajaan Lee Dhammadharo; and my own essay, "A Guided Meditation," included in *Noble Strategy*. If you are not familiar with these instructions, you might want to read through them before reading the talks in this book. Both sets of instructions are available on the Internet at www.accesstoinsight.org. Also, further Dhamma talks are available at www.mettaforest.org.

* * *

I would like to thank Bok Lim Kim for making the recording of these talks possible. She, more than anyone else, is responsible for overcoming my initial reluctance to have the talks taped. I would also like to thank the following people for transcribing the

Introduction

tapes and/or helping to edit the transcriptions: Paul and Debra Breger, Richard Heiman, Jane Yudelman, Dhammattho Bhikkhu, Gunaddho Bhikkhu, Susuddho Bhikkhu, and Khematto Bhikkhu. May they all be happy.

Whatever merit there may be to these talks comes from the training I received from my teachers, Ajaan Fuang Jotiko and Ajaan Suwat Suvaco. This book is dedicated to their memory, with utmost gratitude.

Thanissaro Bhikkhu

Metta Forest Monastery
Valley Center, CA 92082-1409
August, 2003

Generosity First

March, 2003

Several years ago, when Ajaan Suwat was teaching a retreat at IMS, I was his interpreter. After the second or third day of the retreat he turned to me and said, "I notice that when these people meditate they're awfully grim." You'd look out across the room and all the people were sitting there very seriously, their faces tense, their eyes closed tight. It was almost as if they had *Nirvana or Bust* written across their foreheads.

He attributed their grimness to the fact that most people here in the West come to Buddhist meditation without any preparation in other Buddhist teachings. They've had no experience in being generous in line with the Buddha's teachings on giving, no experience in developing virtue in line with the Buddhist precepts. They come to the Buddha's teachings without having tested them in daily life, so they don't have the sense of confidence they need to get them through the hard parts of the meditation. They feel they have to rely on sheer determination instead.

If you look at the way meditation, virtue, and generosity are taught here, it's the exact opposite of the order in which they're taught in Asia. Here, people sign up for a retreat to learn some meditation, and only when they show up at the retreat center do they learn they're going to have to observe some precepts during the retreat. And then at the very end of the retreat they learn that before they'll be allowed to go home they're going to have to be generous. It's all backwards.

Over in Thailand, children's first exposure to Buddhism, after they've learned the gesture of respect, is through giving. You see parents taking their children by the hand as a monk comes past on his alms round, lifting them up, and helping them put a spoonful of rice into the monk's bowl. Over time, as the children start doing it themselves, the process becomes less and less mechanical, and after a while they begin to take pleasure in giving.

At first this pleasure may seem counterintuitive. The idea that you gain happiness by giving things away doesn't come automatically to a young child's mind. But with practice you find that it's true. After all, when you give, you put yourself in a position of wealth. The gift is proof that you have more than enough. At the same time it gives you a sense of your worth as a person. You're able to help other people. The act of giving also creates a sense of spaciousness in the mind, because the world we live in is created by our actions, and the act of giving creates a spacious world: a world where generosity is an operating principle, a world where people have more than enough, enough to share. And it creates a good feeling in the mind.

From there, the children are exposed to virtue: the practice of the precepts. And again, from a child's point of view it's counterintuitive that you're going to be happy by not doing certain things you want to do—as when you want to take something, or when you want to lie to cover up your embarrassment or to protect yourself from criticism and punishment. But over time you begin to discover that, yes, there is a sense of happiness, there is a sense of wellbeing that comes from being principled, from not having to cover up for any lies, from avoiding unskillful actions, from having a sense that unskillful actions are beneath you.

So by the time you come to meditation through the route of giving and being virtuous, you've already had experience in learning that there are counterintuitive forms of happiness in the world. When you've been trained through exposure to the Buddha's teachings, you've learned the deeper happiness that comes from giving, the deeper happiness that comes from restraining yourself from unskillful actions, no matter how much you might want to do them. By the time you come to the meditation you've developed a certain sense of confidence that so far the Buddha has been right, so you give him the benefit of the doubt on meditation.

This confidence is what allows you to overcome a lot of the initial difficulties: the distractions, the pain. At the same time, the spaciousness that comes from generosity gives you the right mindset for the concentration practice, gives you the right mindset for insight practice—because when you sit down and focus on the breath, what kind of mind do you have? The mind you've been creating through your generous and virtuous actions. A spacious mind, not the narrow mind of a person who doesn't have enough. It's the spacious mind of a person who has more than enough to share, the mind of a person who has no regrets or denial over past actions. In short, it's the mind of a person who realizes that true happiness doesn't see a sharp dichotomy between your own wellbeing and the wellbeing of others.

The whole idea that happiness has to consist either in doing things only for your own selfish motives or for other people to the sacrifice of yourself—the dichotomy between the two—is something very Western, but it's antithetical to the Buddha's teachings. According to the Buddha's teachings, true happiness is something that, by its nature, gets spread around. By working for your own true benefit, you're working for the benefit of others. And by working for the benefit of others, you're working for your own. In the act of giving to others you gain rewards. In the act of holding fast to the precepts, holding fast to your principles, protecting others from your unskillful behavior, you gain as well. You gain in mindfulness; you gain in your own sense of worth as a person, your own self-esteem. You protect yourself.

So you come to the meditation ready to apply the same principles to training in tranquility and insight. You realize that the meditation is not a selfish project. You're sitting here trying to understand your greed, anger, and delusion, trying to bring them under control—which means that you're not the only person who's going to benefit from the meditation. Other people will benefit—are benefiting—as well. As you become more mindful, more alert, more skillful in undercutting the hindrances in your mind, other people are less subject to those hindrances as well. Less greed, anger, and delusion come out in your actions, and so the people around you suffer less. Your meditating is a gift to them.

The quality of generosity, what they call *caga* in Pali, is included in many sets of Dhamma teachings. One is the set of practices leading to a fortunate rebirth. This doesn't apply only to the rebirth that comes after death, but also to the states of being, the states of mind you create for yourself moment to moment, that you move into with each moment. You create the world in which you live through your actions. By being generous—not only with material things but also with your time, your energy, your forgiveness, your willingness to be fair and just with other people—you create a good world in which to live. If your habits tend more toward being stingy, they create a very confining world, because there's never enough. There's always a lack of this, or a lack of that, or a fear that something is going to slip away or get taken away from you. So it's a narrow, fearful world you create when you're not generous, as opposed to the confident and wide-open world you create through acts of generosity.

Generosity also counts as one of the forms of Noble Wealth, because what is wealth aside from a sense of having more than enough? Many people who are materially poor are, in terms of their attitude, very wealthy. And many people with a lot of material wealth are extremely poor. The ones who never have enough: They're the ones who always need more security, always need more to stash away. Those are the people who have to build walls around their houses, who have to live in gated communities for fear that other people will take away what they've got. That's a very poor kind of life, a confined kind of life. But as you practice generosity, you realize that you can get by on less, and that there's a pleasure that comes with giving to people. Right there is a sense of wealth. You have more than enough.

At the same time you break down barriers. Monetary transactions create barriers. Somebody hands you something, you have to hand them money back, so there's a barrier right there. Otherwise, if you didn't pay, the object wouldn't come to you over the barrier. But if something is freely given, it breaks down a barrier. You become part of that person's extended family. In Thailand the terms of address that monks use with their lay supporters are the same they use with relatives. The gift of support creates a sense of relatedness. The monastery where I stayed—and this includes the lay supporters as well as the monks—was like a large extended family. This is true of many of the monasteries in Thailand. There's a sense of relatedness, a lack of boundary.

We hear so much talk on "interconnectedness." Many times it's explained in terms of the teaching on dependent co-arising, which is really an inappropriate use of the teaching. Dependent co-arising teaches the connectedness of ignorance to suffering, the connectedness of craving to suffering. That's a connectedness within the mind, and it's a connectedness that we need to cut, because it keeps suffering going on and on and on, over and over again, in many, many cycles. But there's another kind of connectedness, an intentional connectedness, that comes through our actions. These are kamma connections. Now, we in the West often have problems with the teachings on kamma, which may be why we want the teachings on connectedness without the kamma. So we go looking elsewhere in the Buddha's teachings to find a rationale or a basis for a teaching on connectedness, but the real basis for a sense of connectedness comes through kamma. When you interact with another person, a connection is made.

Now, it can be a positive or a negative connection, depending on the intention. With generosity you create a positive connection, a helpful connection, a connection where you're glad that the boundary is down, a connection where good things can flow back and forth. If it's unskillful kamma, you're creating a connection, you're creating an opening that sooner or later you're going to regret. There's a saying in the *Dhammapada* that a hand without a wound can hold poison and not be harmed. In other words, if you don't have any bad kamma, the results of bad kamma won't come to you. But if you have a wound on your hand, then if you hold poison it will seep through the wound and kill you. Unskillful kamma is just that, a wound. It's an opening for poisonous things to come in.

The opposite principle also works. If there's a connection of skillful behavior, a good connection is formed. This sort of positive connection starts with generosity, and grows with the gift of virtue. As the Buddha said, when you hold to your precepts no matter what, with no exceptions, it's a gift of security to all beings. You give unlimited security to everyone, and so you have a share in that unlimited security as well. With the gift of meditation, you protect other people from the effects of your greed, anger, and delusion. And you get protected as well.

So this is what generosity does: It makes your mind more spacious and creates good connections with the people around you. It dissolves the boundaries that otherwise would keep the happiness from spreading around.

When you come to the meditation with that state of mind, it totally changes the way you approach meditating. So many people come to meditation with the question, "What am I going to get out of this time I spend meditating?" Particularly in the modern world, time is something we're very poor in. So the question of getting, getting, getting out of the mediation is always there in the background. We're advised to erase this idea of getting, yet you can't erase it if you've been cultivating it as a habitual part of your mind. But if you come to the meditation with experience in being generous, the question becomes "What do I *give* to the meditation?" You give it your full attention. You give it the effort, you're happy to put in the effort, because you've learned from experience that good effort put into the practice of the Dhamma brings good results. And so that internal poverty of "What am I getting out of this meditation?" gets erased. You come to the meditation with a sense of wealth: "What can I give to this practice?"

You find, of course, that you end up getting a lot more if you start with the attitude of giving. The mind is more up for challenges: "How about if I give it more time? How about meditating later into the night than I usually do? How about getting up earlier in the morning? How about giving more constant attention to what I'm doing? How about sitting longer through pain?" The meditation then becomes a process of giving, and of course you still get the results. When you're not so grudging of your efforts or time, you place fewer and fewer limitations on the process of meditation. That way the results are sure to be less grudging, more unlimited, as well. So it's important that we develop the Noble Wealth of generosity to bring to our meditation.

The texts mention that when you get discouraged in your meditation, when the meditation gets dry, you should look back on past generosity. This gives you a sense of self-esteem, a sense of encouragement. Of course, what generosity are you going to look back on if there is none? This is why it's important that you approach the meditation having practiced generosity very consciously.

Many times we ask, "How do I take the meditation back into the world?" But it's also important that you bring good qualities of the world into your meditation, good qualities of your day-to-day life, and that you develop them regularly. Thinking back on past acts of generosity gets dry after a while if there's only been one act of generosity that happened a long time ago. You need fresh generosity to give you encouragement.

So this is why, when the Buddha talked about the forms of merit, he said, "Don't be afraid of merit, for merit is another word for happiness." The first of the three main forms of merit is *dana,* giving, which is the expression of generosity. The gift of being virtuous builds on the simple act of giving, and the gift of meditation builds on both.

Of course, a large part of the meditation is letting go: letting go of distractions, letting go of unskillful thoughts. If you're used to letting go of material things, it comes a lot easier to begin experimenting with letting go of unskillful mental attitudes—things that you've held on to for so long that you think you need them, but when you really look at them you find you don't. In fact, you see that they're an unnecessary burden that causes suffering. When you see the suffering, and the fact that it's needless, you can let go. In this way, the momentum of giving carries all the way through the practice, and you realize that it's not depriving you of anything. It's more like a trade. You give away a material object and you gain in generous qualities of mind. You give away your defilements, and you gain freedom.

The How & the Why

November 14, 1996

Two important questions you have to answer about meditation are "how?" and "why?"—how to do it and why you are doing it—because meditation is not just a technique. There's a context for the practice, and only when you see the practice in context can you really understand what you're doing and get the most out of it.

The "how" is pretty simple. With breath meditation, sit straight, hands in your lap, right hand on top of your left hand, your legs crossed, right leg on top of the left leg, your eyes closed. That's getting your body into position. Getting your mind into position means focusing it in on the present moment. Think about the breath and then notice how the breath feels as it comes in, how it feels as it goes out. Be aware of the breathing. That means you have two qualities at work: the thinking or mindfulness, which reminds you where to stay; and the alertness, which tells you what's happening with the breath. Those are two of the qualities you want.

The third quality is what the Buddha called *atappa,* or ardency, which means you really put an effort into it. You really focus on what you're doing. You're not just playing around. You give it your whole attention. You try to be ardently mindful and ardently alert.

Ardently mindful means that you try to keep your mindfulness as continuous as possible, without any gaps. If you find that your mind has slipped off the breath, you bring it right back. You don't let it dawdle here or sniff at the flowers there. You've got work to do and you want to get it done as quickly, as thoroughly, as possible. You have to maintain that kind of attitude. As the Buddha said, it's like realizing that your head is on fire. You put it out as fast as possible. The issues we're dealing with are serious issues, urgent issues: aging, illness, and death. They're like fires burning away inside us.

So you have to maintain that sense of ardency because you never know when these fires are going to flare up. You want to be as prepared as possible, as quickly as possible. So when the mind wanders off, be ardent in bringing it back.

Ardently alert means that when the mind is staying with the breath, you try to be as sensitive as possible in adjusting it to make it feel good, and in monitoring the results of your efforts. Try long breathing to see how it feels. Try short breathing, heavy breathing, light breathing, deep, shallow. The more refined you can make your awareness, the better the meditation goes because you can make the breath more and more refined, a more and more comfortable place for the mind to stay. Then you can let that sense of comfort spread throughout the body. Think of the breath not simply as the air coming in and out the lungs, but as the flow of energy throughout the whole body. The more refined your awareness, the more sensitive you can be to that flow. The more sensitive you are, the more refined the breath becomes, the more gratifying, the more absorbing it becomes as a place to stay.

This is the basic trick in getting the mind to settle down in the present moment—you've got to give it something that it likes to stay with. If it's here against its will, it's going to be like a balloon you push under the water. As long as your hand has a good grasp on the balloon, it's not going to pop up, but as soon as you slip a little bit, the balloon pops up out of the water. If the mind is forced to stay on an object that it really finds unpleasant, it's not going to stay. As soon as your mindfulness slips just a little bit, it's gone.

Or you can compare it to parents raising a child. If the parents are constantly beating the child, the child is going to run away from home as soon as it finds the chance. Even if they lock the windows and doors, it's going to look for an opening. As soon as they turn their backs, it's gone. But if the parents are kind to the child—give it good things to play with, interesting things to do at home, lots of warmth and love—the child will want to stay home even if the windows and doors are left wide open.

So it is with the mind. Be friendly with it. Give it something good to stay with in the present moment—like comfortable breathing. Maybe you can't make the whole body comfortable, but make at least part of the body comfortable and stay with that part. As for the pains, let them be in the other part. They have every right to be there, so make an arrangement with them. They stay in one part, you stay in another. But the essential point is that you have a place where the mind feels stable, secure, and comfortable in the present moment. These are the beginning steps in meditation.

This kind of meditation can be used for all sorts of purposes, but the Buddha realized that the most important purpose is to get the mind out of the whole cycle of aging, illness, and death. And when you think about it, there's nothing more important than that. That's the big problem in life and yet society tends to slough off the problems of aging, illness, and death, tends to push them off to the side because other things seem more pressing. Making a lot of money is more important. Having fulfilling relationships is more important. Whatever. And the big issues in life—the fact that you're headed for the sufferings and indignities that come with an aging, ill, or dying body—get pushed off, pushed out of the way. "Not yet, not yet, maybe some other time." And of course when that other time does arrive and these things come barging in, they won't accept your "not yet," won't be pushed out anymore. If you haven't prepared yourself for them, you'll really be up the creek, at a total loss.

So these are the most important things you need to prepare for. A lot of other things in life are uncertain, but a couple of things are certain. Aging comes. Illness comes. Death is going to come for sure. So when you know something is going to come for sure, you have to prepare for it. And when you realize that this is the most important issue in life, you have to look at the way you live your life. Meditation—the practice of the Buddha's teachings— is not just a question of sitting with your eyes closed every now and then. It's about how you order your priorities. As the Buddha said, when you see there's a greater level of happiness that can be found by sacrificing lesser forms of happiness, you sacrifice the lesser ones. Look at your life and the things you hold onto, the little places where the mind finds its pleasure but doesn't gain any real fulfillment: Are those the things you really want to hold onto? Are you going to let them be the factors governing your life?

And then you can think of larger issues. The chance for a happiness that goes beyond aging, illness, and death: Will that be the first priority in your life?

These are questions we all have to ask within ourselves. The Buddha doesn't force our answers. He simply sets out what the situation is. He says that there is a possibility for happiness lying beyond the happiness that comes from simply eating and sleeping, looking after the body and having a comfortable time. This possibility is the good news in the Buddha's teachings, especially since most of the world says, "Well, this is all there is to life, so make the most of it. Satisfy yourself with these immediate pleasures and don't think about other things. Don't let yourself get dissatisfied with what you've got." When you think about this attitude, it's really depressing because all it means is that you grab at what you can before you die. And when you die, you can't take it with you.

But the Buddha said there's a form of happiness, there's a form of knowing in the mind, that goes beyond aging, illness, and death, and that can be attained through human effort if you're skillful enough. So that's both good news and a challenge. Are you going to let yourself just live an ordinary life frittering your time away? Or are you going to accept the challenge to devote yourself to more important things, devote yourself to this possibility?

The Buddha was the sort of person who put his life on the line. He didn't have anyone telling him that this was a possibility, but he thought that the only way life would have any dignity, any honor would be if you could find a happiness that doesn't age, doesn't grow ill, doesn't die. And he ran up against all the things he would have to sacrifice in order to find that happiness. So he made those sacrifices—not because he wanted to sacrifice those things, but because he had to. As a result he was able to find what he was looking for. So the story of his life and his teachings are meant as a challenge for us—how are we going to lead *our* lives?

Here we are sitting together meditating. What are you going to do with a still mind, once it's become still? If you wanted to, you could simply use concentration practice as a method of relaxation or a way of calming the nerves. However, the Buddha says that there's more to it than that. When the mind is really still, you can dig deep down into the mind and begin to see all the currents that lie underground within it. You can start sorting them out, understanding what drives the mind. Where is the greed? Where is the anger? Where are the delusions that keep you spinning around? How can you cut through them?

These are the questions, these are the issues that can be tackled in the meditation—as long as you have a sense of their importance, that they're your real priorities. If you don't have that sense, you don't want to touch them because they're big issues and they snarl at you when you get near. But if you really dig down, you find that they're just paper tigers. I once saw a meditation manual that contained a drawing of a tiger. The face of a tiger was very realistic—all the details were very scary—but its body was made out of folded paper. And that's what a lot of issues are in the mind. They come at you, looking really intimidating, but if you face them down they turn into origami.

But in order to face them down you've got to have a sense that these are the really important issues in life and you're willing to give up an awful lot for their sake. You're willing to give up whatever you have to give up. That's what makes the difference between a practice that goes someplace, that really knocks down the walls in the mind, and a practice that simply rearranges the furniture in the room.

So when you practice meditation, you realize there is both the "how" and the "why," and the "why" is really important. Often the "why" gets pushed off to the side. You simply follow this or that technique, and then what you want to do with it is up to you—which is true in a way, but doesn't take into account the possibilities. When you put the possibilities into the context of the

Buddha's teachings, you see the values that underlie the practice. You see how deep the practice goes, how much it can accomplish, and what an enormous job you're taking on. It's enormous, but the results are enormous as well.

And the issues are urgent. Aging, illness, and death can come at any time, and you have to ask yourself, "Are you prepared? Are you ready to die?" Ask yourself in all honesty and if you're not ready, what's the problem? What are you still lacking? Where are you still holding on? Why do you want to hold on? When the mind settles down and is still, you can start digging into these issues. And the more you dig, the more you uncover within the mind—layers and layers of things that you didn't suspect, that have been governing your life since who knows when. You dig them out, you see them for what they are, and you're free from them. You realize all the stupid things that have been running your life, picked up from who knows where. You can't blame anyone else. You're the one who picked them up and you played along with them.

Now, when you realize that nothing is accomplished by playing along—that it's better not to play along with these things, and you don't have to—then you can let them go. And they let *you* go. What's left is total freedom. The Buddha said that it's so total it can't even be described by words.

So that's the possibility the meditation points to, and it's up to each of us to decide how far we want to go in that direction, how much we do really care for our true happiness, for our own true wellbeing. You would think that everyone would say, "Of course I care for my happiness and true wellbeing." But if you look at the way people live their lives, you can see that they really don't put that much energy or thought into the quest for true happiness. People usually see other people do things in this or that way, so they follow along without looking for themselves, as if true happiness were so unimportant that you could leave it up to other people to make your choices for you. Meditation, though, is a chance to look for yourself at what's really important in life and then do something about it.

Watch What You're Doing

August 19, 2003

"Days and nights fly past, fly past: What am I doing right now?"

The Buddha has you ask that question every day, both to keep yourself from being complacent and to remind yourself that the practice is one of *doing*. Even though we're sitting here very still, there's still a doing going on in the mind. There's the intention to focus on the breath, the intention to maintain that focus, and the intention to keep watch over how the breath and the mind are behaving. Meditation as a whole is a doing. Even when you practice non-reactivity or "being the knowing," there's a still an element of intention. That's what the doing is.

That was one of the Buddha's most important insights: that even when you're sitting perfectly still with the intention not to do anything, there's still the intention, and the intention itself is a doing. It's a *sankhara,* a fabrication. It's what we live with all the time. In fact, all of our experience is based on fabrication. The fact that you sense your body, feelings, perceptions, thought-fabrications, consciousness—all of these aggregates: To be able to experience them in the present moment you have to fabricate a potential into an actual aggregate. You fabricate the potential for form into an actual experience of form, the potential for feeling into an actual experience of feeling, and so on. This element of fabrication lies in the background all the time. It's like the background noise of the Big Bang, which hums throughout the whole universe and doesn't go away. The element of fabrication is always there, shaping our experience, and it's so consistently present that we lose sight of it. We don't realize what we're doing.

What you're trying to do as you meditate is to strip things down so you can see the very elemental fabrications going on in the mind, the kamma you're creating with every moment. We're not making the mind still simply to have a nice restful place to be, a nice experience of ease to soothe our stressed-out nerves. That may be part of it, but it's not the whole practice. The other part is to see clearly what's going on, to see the potential of human action: What are we doing all the time? What are the potentials contained in this doing? Then we apply that understanding of human action to see how far we can go in stripping away the unnecessary stress and suffering that come from acting in unskillful ways.

It's important that we always keep this in mind as we meditate. Remember: We're here to understand human action, in particular our own human actions. Otherwise we sit here hoping that we don't have to do anything, that we can just wait for some Imax experiences to come whap us upside the head, or some nice glowing sense of oneness to come welling up inside. And sometimes things like that *can* come unexpectedly, but if they come without your understanding how or why they came, they're not all that helpful. They're restful for a while, or amazing for a while, but then they go away and you have to deal with your desire to get them back. And, of course, no amount of desire is going to get them back if it's not accompanied by understanding.

You can't totally drop human action until you understand the nature of action. This is really important. We like to think that we can simply stop doing, stop doing, stop doing, and things will settle down, get calm, and open up to emptiness. But that's more like zoning out than meditating. There *is* an element of stopping in the meditation, an element of letting go, but you can't really master it until you understand what you're trying to stop, what you're letting go. So try to watch out for that. When you come out of a good meditation, don't simply get up and go back to the kitchen, have a cocoa, and go back to sleep. Reflect on what you did so as to understand the pattern of cause and effect, to see exactly what you fabricated in the process of bringing the mind down to a state of calm. After all, the path *is* a fabricated path. It's the ultimate fabrication. As the Buddha said, of all the fabricated phenomena there are in the world, the highest is the noble eightfold path. This is the path we're trying to follow right now. It's something put together, and you won't understand it until you see the putting-together as you're doing it.

So always have that in the back of your mind: that you are doing something here. Sometimes it seems frustrating that the whole hour may be spent just pulling back, pulling back, pulling the mind back to the breath. It wanders off, so you pull it back again, and then it wanders—*when* is the peace and calm going to come? Well, before it can come you have to develop some understanding. So when you pull it back, try to understand what you're doing. When it wanders off, try to understand what's happening, what you did to encourage or allow it to wander off. In particular, try to uncover all the skillful and unskillful intentions that go into this back-and-forth process. When you understand how the mind goes back and forth, you'll reach the point where you can keep it from going back and forth. At the same time, you'll develop the kind of insight we want in the meditation: insight into actions.

The Buddha said discernment involves comprehending the process of fabrication, the process of action that's going on in the mind all the time. And all the basic building blocks of action are right here. There's the physical fabrication that leads to action—in other words, the breath. Without the breath you couldn't do any other physical actions at all. Then there's verbal fabrication: directed thought and evaluation. Without those you wouldn't be able to speak. And then there's mental fabrication: perceptions and feelings. Without those, the process of mental fabrication wouldn't have any building blocks to build with. These are all the most basic forms of activity: physical, verbal, and mental. So we bring them all together right here when we've got the mind with the breath. We're focused on the breath, directing our thoughts to the breath, evaluating the breath, aware of all the mental labels that label the breath, and all the feelings that come with the breath, pleasant or unpleasant. All the basic building blocks are right here.

These building blocks are not things, they're activities. You might call them basic activity units. These are the things you have to bring together in order to get the mind to settle down. Otherwise it goes off and elaborates all kinds of other worlds to inhabit, pulling its attention away from the basic activity units and hoping to live in their end-products. So you keep reminding yourself to come back to this level, this level, this level where things are basic. You try to manipulate these things skillfully so as to still the mind. It's an intentional stilling, so there's an element of doing even in the being still, but it's a doing for the purpose of knowing. Most of our doing is for the purpose of ignorance. It comes out of ignorance and heads toward ignorance, covering up our intentions so that we can forget the effort that goes into the doing and simply enjoy the end-product experiences that our doing creates.

Some people think that Buddhism is a religion of experiences. We want to have a religious experience when we come here, we want to have an experience of release or an experience of peace. Actually, though, the Dhamma is meant to take us beyond our incessant habit of producing and consuming experiences. And to do that, we have to understand the nature of action that underlies the producing and consuming, to see exactly what it is to be a human being who acts. What does it mean to act? How does the mind act? What is an intention? Why does the mind have intentions? Are these processes really pleasant, or are they burdensome? What would it be like if we didn't have to do them? We need to look into these things, we need to understand these processes before we can get to where we really want to go. If you don't understand human action, you won't be able to explore the full limits of human action. You won't be able to understand how far human action can take you. So we're here to study, we're here to learn from our actions.

This teaching on action is something particular to the Buddha's teachings—this sense of what an action is and how far an action can go. It's easy to say that all the great religions focus on having experiences beyond what words can describe. Sounds nice. Very friendly. Very ecumenical. But when you compare what the various religions say about action—what it means to act, what the potentials of human action are—you see that they differ greatly. Some teachings say that we don't really act at all, that there's an outside force acting through us, that everything's pre-determined. Others say that we do act, but our actions have no real consequences. Or that there are lots of limitations on what we can do to produce true happiness, so we need some outside power to help us. You can't lump these various teachings on action together and pretend that the differences don't count. The fact is: They don't jibe. They're diametrically opposed. They get in one another's way.

This was why the early Buddhists kept insisting that the teaching on action was what set Buddhism apart, that it was the most important issue where people have to make a choice and take a stand. And this was why the Buddha's last words were that we need to be heedful. He didn't end his teaching career with some nice platitudes on emptiness or nibbana. He said to be heedful—to see our actions as important and to keep that importance in mind at all times.

So this is where you have to make a choice: Which theory of action are you planning to place your hopes on? That's what you're asked to commit to when you take refuge in the Triple Gem: the teaching on action, the teaching on kamma. Taking refuge is not a warm, fuzzy, cowardly cop-out. It's the act of taking on full responsibility for your choices and intentions. How far are you planning to go with your actions? How far are you willing to push the envelope? These are questions that we all have to answer for ourselves, and no one can force the answer on us. But just remember: The Buddha said that it's possible for human action to go to the end of action—in other words, to go to a dimension in the mind where ultimately there is no more intention. He says that that's the highest happiness. Now, we can take that statement merely as an historical curiosity or we can take that as a personal challenge. It's up to us.

At the very least, when you're sitting here meditating and things don't seem to be going right, don't blame it on the weather. Don't blame it on the time of day. Just look at what you're doing. Look at the raw material you have to work with and your skill in fashioning that raw material into a state of calm. From the Buddhist point of view, that raw material comes from past actions. You can't change the fact that this is the raw material you have at hand, but you *can* fashion that raw material in different ways. That freedom of choice is always present. So if things aren't going well in your meditation, look at your intentions to see what you might change. Look at your perceptions, at the questions you're posing in the mind. Experiment. Improvise. See what makes a difference.

When things *are* going well, try to maintain them well. See how you can develop that sense of wellness even further. This is Right Effort. This is where we encounter the element of intention, the element of action directly in our own minds. If you sit here complaining about how things aren't going well in your meditation, that's your choice: You chose to complain. Is that the most skillful thing to do? If it's not, try something else. You've always got that freedom.

When things are going well, you can always choose to get complacent. If you get complacent, where does that take you? You can choose to manipulate things too much, too little, or just right. The choices are here. It's important that we keep that in mind. Otherwise we find ourselves trapped in a particular situation and can't think our way out, because we don't realize the range of available possibilities.

Try to keep your sense of those possibilities as alive as possible, so that the doing of the meditation becomes a skillful doing and not just a thrashing around. You observe, you watch, you look into this question: "What does it mean to have an intention? How can I see the results of my intentions? Where do they show their results?" They show their results both in your state of mind and in your breathing, so look right here, make your adjustments right here.

And even if you're not consciously thinking about the nature of human action, you're learning a lot about your own actions as you work with the breath, trying to keep the mind with the breath, trying to make the breath a good place for the mind to stay. You're muddling around here in the basic elements of human action, like a young kid fooling around with a guitar: After a while, if the kid is observant, the fooling around turns into music. The more observant you are in the way you relate to the breath, the more your muddle will turn into a process of discovery.

The Interactive Present

August, 2002

When you try to settle into the present moment, sometimes you find sticks, rocks, and thorns. They can be either in the body or in the mind, and you have to do your best to deal with them. It would be nice if you could simply follow some easy, step-by-step instructions: 1,2,3,4, first you do this and then you do that, and then the results come without your having to figure anything out on your own. And sometimes there *are* instructions like that in meditation books—but often the mind doesn't fall in line with them. Ideally you should be able to let the mind settle down and grow calm and *then* deal with difficult issues, but sometimes before you can settle down you've got to deal with some difficulties first.

It's not only the case that discernment requires concentration. Concentration also requires discernment—learning how to bypass whatever issues you can bypass and how to deal directly with the ones you have to deal with before you can get the mind to settle down.

If there's rampant lust or anger in the mind, you've got to deal with it. You can't pretend it's not there. You can't shove it off into the corner, for it'll keep jumping out of the corner back at you. So you remind yourself of the drawbacks of that kind of thinking; you look to see where there's a lack of reasoning or a lack of logic in that kind of thinking. Many times that thinking simply comes at you with a lot of force, just as a belligerent person comes at you with a lot of force to make up for his lack of reason.

So you look at your lust, look at your anger, look at your fears, and try to see, "What are they actually saying?" Sometimes you have to listen to them. If you listen really carefully you'll see that after a while they don't make any sense. When you can see that, it's a lot easier to put them aside. When they come back at you, say, "You're not making any sense at all." Then you've got a handle on them.

The same with physical pain. Sometimes when you sit down to meditate there's pain in the body and it has nothing to do with the meditation posture. It's simply there no matter what your posture. So you have to learn how to deal with it. Focus on other parts of the body so you get at least *some* sense of having a beachhead in the present moment, a place where you can stay and you're okay. Then you work from that position of strength. Once you get a sense of the breath going smoothly and comfortably, you let it expand from that spot into other parts of the body, moving through the part where there's pain and out the feet and out the hands.

You begin to realize that those thorns in the present are *not* just a given. There has to be a part of you that's playing along with them, that's making them a problem. Once you see that, the thorns are a lot easier to deal with.

Sometimes there's a pain in the body and the way you're breathing is actually maintaining it. Sometimes the problem is your fear that it's going to spread, which makes you build a little shell of tension around it—and while that shell of tension may keep the pain from spreading, it also keeps it in existence. The breath energy doesn't flow smoothly there, and that helps maintain the pain. When you catch yourself doing this, you get an interesting insight: The present moment is not just something given. You're participating in it. An element of your intention is shaping it.

Then you can turn around and use this same principle with the mind. When there's lust or anger, part of it may be coming from past habit, but another part from your present participation. It's easy to understand this in the case of lust. You're enjoying it and so you want to continue it. Actually, part of the mind is enjoying it while another part is suffering. What you want to do is bring the suffering part out, give it voice, give it some space to express itself.

This is especially needed in our culture. People who don't submit to their lust are said to be repressed and have all kinds warped beasts in the basement. So the part of the mind that thrives when it's freed from lust doesn't get a chance. *It* gets pushed into the corner of the basement. *It* becomes the repressed part. But if you can ferret out the part of the mind that's really enjoying the lust and say: "Hey, wait a minute, what kind of enjoyment is this? How about that stress over there? How about that discomfort over there? The sense of dissatisfaction that comes along with the lust, the cloudiness that comes into the mind because of the lust—how about that?" You can start to highlight the part of the mind that really doesn't enjoy the lust. Then you have a better chance of dealing with the lust and working your way out from under its thumb.

The same with anger: Try to find the part of the mind that's enjoying the anger. See what kind of happiness it gets from indulging in the anger. See how piddling and miserable that happiness is. That way you strengthen the part of the mind that really doesn't want to play along.

The same goes with other emotions, such as fear or greed: Once you catch the part of the mind that's enjoying it—participating, keeping it going right now—learn to undercut it. Learn how to emphasize the part that doesn't want to play along.

Then you can start applying the same principle to positive mind states, the ones that you're trying to develop. If you're conscious of the part of the mind that doesn't want to stay with the breath, try to find the part of the mind that does, that really appreciates having a chance to settle down and let go of its burdens. The potential is there, simply that it's not emphasized.

So learn to give yourself pep talks. People who get easily discouraged are the ones who haven't learned that talent. You have to learn how to give yourself encouragement: "See? You did that. You brought the mind back. See if you can do it again the next time. See if you can do it faster." That's the kind of encouragement you need, the kind that keeps you participating in getting states of concentration going. After all, if the present isn't just a given, why don't you learn how to shape a good present? Emphasize the positive things, so they really do get stronger. That way you find that you're less and less a victim of events. You come to play a stronger, more positive role in shaping your experience of the present.

We talk many times about how ultimately you want to discontinue that participation in the present so that you can open up to the Deathless. But before you do that, you've got to get skillful in how you participate in the present moment. You can't skip straight from unskillful participation to the ultimate skill of learning how to open up to the Deathless. You've got to go through all of the stages of learning how to make the present a more positive experience— through the way you breathe, the way you focus on the breath, the way you deal with the various states, positive or negative, that come up in the mind. You've got to learn how to be a better manager of the present moment before you can develop the even more refined skills of learning how to take all of this participation apart.

So when you sit down to meditate, you've got to realize that not everything is a given. You're participating right now. What kind of participation do you want to develop? What kind of participation do you want to discontinue, to drop?

These pains—the stones and thorns and all the other things that make it hard to settle down: They're not just a given. Your element of participation helps create the stones, helps sharpen the thorns. If you can catch yourself doing that and can unlearn the habit, you find it a lot easier to settle down and stay settled. You can see more clearly what's going on, and your skill in dealing with the present gets more and more refined.

Imagine

April 20, 2003

Psychologists have done studies of people who've mastered skills, trying to figure out why some people are simply very good at a particular skill while other people really master it. One of their discoveries is that for people to really master a skill, it has to capture their imagination. They like to think about it. They like to try different ways of conceptualizing the skill, approaching the skill, applying the skill in unusual and unexpected ways. And although we often don't think of imagination as being involved in meditation—in fact, we think that meditation is anti-imagination—actually that's not the case. To master concentration, it has to capture your imagination, just as with any other skill.

When you practice concentration, what are you doing? You're creating a state in the mind. That requires imagination. The noble eightfold path as a whole is something fabricated, something put together. It brings you into the present, but when you get into the present you discover how much input your intentions have in each present moment. The practice of the path is designed to make you more and more sensitive to that fact: to see how you put things together, how you can put things together in a way that creates suffering, or how you can get more skillful at putting things together in a way that creates less and less suffering until finally you reach a point where the whole thing gets taken apart and there's no suffering left.

But to get to that last point you have to understand what you're doing. You can't simply make up your mind that you're going to be totally uninvolved in the present moment and simply be an observer without participating, because what happens is that your participation goes underground. You don't see it, but it's still there. So, instead, you have to be very open about the fact that you're shaping the present moment simply by choosing what you focus on. That's a decision right there: The sensations you choose to focus on, and the way you focus on them, are going to shape your experience of the present moment. You're creating a state of becoming—the Pali word here is *bhava*—and although one of the things we're trying to learn to overcome is the process of becoming, we can't simply drop the process. We have to understand it before we can let it go. We have to understand it to the point of dispassion and then let go. To do that we have to keep creating more and more and more of these states, but we have to create a type of state that's comfortable to stay with, easy to analyze, easy to take apart—which is why we practice concentration.

A senior monk in Bangkok once asked Ajaan Lee, "When you're practicing concentration, aren't you creating states of becoming in the mind?" And Ajaan Lee responded, "Yes, that's precisely what you're doing." He went on to say that you can't take the process apart until you can do it really well. He said, "It's like having a hen that lays eggs. You use some of the eggs to eat, while the others you crack open and take apart." In other words, part of the role of concentration is to keep the mind nourished on the path. The other part is to give you something to take apart, while at the same time putting the mind in a position where it can take these present states apart.

So when you're conscious of that fact, look at the way you put the present moment together. You have choices you know: different things you can focus on, different ways you can focus on them. If you focus on the breath, you discover that there are many different ways of conceiving and monitoring the breath: your way of labeling the breath sensations, the way you decide when an in-breath is long enough, when it's too long, when it's too short. A lot of these decisions get put on automatic pilot, but as you're meditating you have a chance to examine them. You can look at them carefully and adjust them to see if there are more skillful ways of deciding how long a good long in-breath is, what signs indicate that the breath is just long enough. The same holds true with the out-breaths, the depth, the rhythm, the texture of the breath.

There's a lot to play with here, and the word "play" is important because you've got to enjoy the process. Otherwise there's no enthusiasm for the meditation; you simply go through the motions because it's time to meditate. And when there's no enthusiasm, no joy in the process, you have a hard time sticking with it. The mind is going to lose interest, get bored and try to find something else to think about, something else to fill up the hour. And what you end up doing is filling up the hour with filler—straw, shredded paper, and Styrofoam peanuts—things that are not nearly as helpful as learning about the breath. The reason we're here is not just to put in time. We're here to see how the mind is creating unnecessary suffering for itself and to learn how to stop doing it.

One helpful way of understanding the process is to look at the ways psychologists have analyzed imagination. They've discovered that it involves four skills. The first is being able to generate an image in the mind—simply giving rise to an image of one kind or another. The second is to maintain the image. The third is to inspect it, look at its details, explore some of its ramifications. And then the fourth ability is to alter the image, making changes and then inspecting it again to see what happens as you alter it. And although the psychologists who discovered these four skills were concerned primarily with mental pictures in the mind, you'll discover that any kind of creative work—writing, creating a tune, whatever—involves these same four steps.

When you compare the four steps to concentration, you find that they apply here as well. In fact, they correspond to the four bases of success: desire, persistence, intentness, and ingenuity.

In terms of concentration, the first step corresponds to giving rise to a nice pleasant state right here in the present moment. Can you do that? If you want to, you can. As the Buddha said, all phenomena are rooted in desire. So how are you going to make use of desire to give rise to to that pleasant state? You can adjust the breath. You can adjust your focus. Breathe in such a way that gives rise to a pleasant feeling in at least one part of the body.

Then the next step, once you've learned how to generate that state, is to maintain it, keep it going. And you'll discover that you need mindfulness, alertness, steadiness to do that. Sometimes you find that it's like surfing: The wave changes beneath you, but you learn to keep your balance. In other words, the needs of the body will change, but you can keep that pleasant sensation going in spite of those changes. When you first sit down, the body may need a fairly heavy rate of breathing in order to feel comfortable, but then as it feels more comfortable, the body's needs will change. And so you have to learn how to ride that change in the wave. Adjust the rate of breathing so that it's just right for the body right now, right now, right now. This makes you more and more sensitive to the fact that the body's needs change, but you can learn how to maintain a particular balance as you get more and more sensitive in responding to those needs, in giving the body the kind of breathing it wants. Of course, the body's not going to sit there saying, "I want this. I want that," but you get more and more sensitive to the signs, the sensations that tell you that certain parts of the body are starved of breath energy, and you can consciously breathe into them.

The third step is inspection. You look at the state you have in the body: Are there places where it's still uncomfortable, places where it still feels tense, where it feels tight? Well, you can think of ways to change the breath. That's the fourth step. The third and fourth steps play off each other in this way: Once you change things, you inspect them again to see if the change has made any improvement or if it's made things worse. If it's made things worse, you can try another change. Keep inspecting, keep adjusting. In Pali this is called *vicara,* or evaluation. And as things get more and more comfortable, you find that the range of comfort you've been able to create for yourself begins to expand. You can breathe in with a sense that the breath energy in the body is connected in all its parts. You breathe out and the energy feels connected; your awareness keeps filling the body, saturating the body.

After a while you get to a point where you really can't improve the breath any further. It's just right as it is. As Ajaan Fuang once said, it's like pouring water into a water jar. You finally reach the point where you've filled the jar and no matter how much water you try to add after that, you can't get it any fuller than that. So you stop adding water. The same with the breath: When you reach the point of fullness, you stop making so many adjustments, so many changes. You can just be with the breathing. From this point on it's more a question of how the mind relates to the breath, whether it feels that it's separate from the breath and watching it, or whether it's more immersed in the breathing. As it gets more immersed, the rate of breathing is going to change, not so much because you made up your mind to change it, but simply because you've changed your relationship to the breath.

As you get more fully immersed in the body and breath, you develop a sturdy feeling of unification and ease. The breathing will grow more subtle to the point where it finally stops, not because you've forced it to stop but because the mind has slowed down enough to the point where it needs less and less and less oxygen. The oxygen exchange at the skin is enough to keep the body going so that it doesn't have to keep pumping in, pumping out. Ajaan Lee compares this state to an ice cube with vapor coming off of it: The body feels very still, but around the edges there's a kind of effortless vapor that you feel with the in-and-out breathing. Then after a while even that stops and everything is perfectly still.

All of this comes from creating that spot in the body where it feels good to stay focused. Then learning how to maintain it. Then inspecting it to see where you can expand it, where you can make it more stable. And then adjusting it in various ways: using your imagination to think at least of the possibility that the breath could be more comfortable, the breath could saturate the body. You could think of all the cells of the body being bathed in the breath—whatever way you have of conceiving the breath that makes it more and more comfortable, a better and better place to stay.

In this way the four aspects of imagination apply to what you're doing right here, even though you're not trying to create a mental picture. Sometimes there *will* be mental pictures behind it, but you're more concerned with the actual sensation of the breath as you feel it coming in, as you feel it going out, as you play with it, as you create a sense of very intense wellbeing right here. Even though it's something created, something fabricated, it's a good thing to create, a good thing to fabricate. As the Buddha said, right concentration is the heart of the path. The other factors are its requisites. And for discernment to do its work of insight in the present moment, the heart of the path has to stay healthy and strong. You have to create and maintain a good solid basis through concentration.

So because it's a created state, you have to be creative about it, imaginative about it. And you find that the more your imagination opens up to the possibilities already present, the more new possibilities your imagination opens up. As long as you're frank about the process, that you're creating this state, you don't have to worry about getting attached to it—even though you probably will get attached to it—because deep down inside you know it's something you've created, and eventually you'll have to take it apart. But in the mean time, learn how to do it well. The more solid the concentration, the more you want to stay here. The more you stay here, the more familiar you get with the territory. And it's through that familiarity that the practice of concentration turns into the practice of insight, the kind of insight that can liberate you. Without this stability and familiarity, your insights are simply ideas you've heard from Dhamma talks, read in books, notions you've picked up from outside. They don't seep deep into the mind because the mind hasn't softened up the territory here in the present moment. Only through the practice of concentration can the hardness in the present moment begin to soften up and give the insights a chance to seep deeper and deeper.

So when you have this kind of understanding about what you're doing, you find it a lot easier to go about it. And you begin to realize it's not a mechanical process. It's a creative process. That way it can capture your imagination. When it captures your imagination, you get more interested in what you can do with the breath, not just when you're sitting here with your eyes closed, but any time of the day. How you deal with the breath, how you get centered in the breath, can help you deal with anger. It makes you more sensitive to what anger does to the body, and you can breathe through the physical manifestations of the anger so that you don't feel like they've taken over.

When there's fear, you can try using the breath to deal with fear. Get in touch with the physical side of the fear and breathe right through it. Notice how the breath can help deal with boredom, how it can help deal with illness, how it can help deal with pain. There's a lot to explore here. And as the possibilities of the breath capture your imagination, you find that this skill is useful, not only when you're trying to sit with your eyes closed, but also wherever the present may be, wherever you may be in the present. Whatever the context, whatever the situation, you find that the breath has something to offer—if you explore it. And to explore it, you have to get a sense that it can capture your imagination. It gives you that kind of challenge, along with the sense of reward that comes when you've explored something and discovered something new, a valuable skill.

This is how meditation can start permeating your whole life. When it permeates your whole life, when you're more and more familiar with it, that's when the insights arise: unexpected insights sometimes, insights that you won't always find in the books, but very personal, very much relevant to how you relate to events in the body and mind. And you realize that they've come to you because you've opened up your imagination to what's possible with the raw materials of the present.

In the Mood

November 23, 2002

Ajaan Suwat often recommended putting yourself in a good mood each time before you meditate. This may sound a little backwards for many of us because we meditate in order to put ourselves in a good mood, and yet he says to start out with a good mood. But when you stop to think about it, there's really no way you can get good results out of the meditation unless the mind has at least some good qualities in it, some cheerfulness, some patience, some wisdom. These are qualities that act as seeds, that allow the meditation to develop. We're not totally empty-handed when we come to the meditation. We do have good qualities in the mind, and there are plenty of things we can think about to put the mind in a good mood.

This is why we have the chant on goodwill to start out the meditation each and every time. Goodwill is a good thing to think about. You look at yourself spreading thoughts of goodwill and you feel good about yourself. You're not totally selfish, not totally angry, vindictive, whatever. There's at least *some* goodness inside you. You take that as your starting capital. As with any investment, you need to have something to begin with. If you don't have money, at least you've got strength, or you've got your intelligence. You take whatever good things you've got and you invest them. That's how they grow.

So when we sit here to meditate we do our best to make the mind patient, to lift it above its ordinary cares and concerns of the day, and then bring it to the meditation object. That way you can relate to the breath, or whatever your object, in a friendly way.

Being in a good mood puts the breath in good shape as well. If you feel frustrated about your breathing or frustrated about your meditation, that's going to do funny things to your breath, make it harder and harder to stay with the breath. So think in whatever way helps the mind get ready to meditate, in the mood to meditate. This is part of the first basis of success: *chanda,* the desire to meditate. You want to meditate. You feel an inclination, an attraction to the meditation.

If you sit down and you feel yourself totally disinclined to meditate, don't just force yourself to do it. Remind yourself of the good reasons for why you're doing it. Think of ways to make it interesting, ways to make it entertaining. You can do all kinds of things with the breath. Look at Ajaan Lee's Dhamma talks: When he defines the different levels of breathing in the body, he hardly ever repeats himself. There's always something new, something different that he's found from his meditation. We don't have to memorize all his ways of analyzing the breath. We should give them a try, of course, but we should also look at *our* ways of analyzing the breath energy and see what works for us. When you feel depressed, what kind of breathing feels uplifting and energizing? When you feel manic, what kind of breathing feels grounding? When you feel lazy, what kind of breathing energizes you? When you feel tense, what kind of breathing relaxes you? There's a lot to explore, and in the exploration you get absorbed in the breath without even thinking about forcing yourself or holding a whip over the mind.

This way the mind can be on good terms with the breath, the breath can be good, and it's easier and easier to settle down. So always take stock of your mind before you meditate, to see what kind of shape it's in.

Don't let thoughts of frustration or discouragement take charge of the mind. The Dalai Lama once said that the thing he found most surprising about Westerners was their self-hatred. In Tibet, he said, only the village idiots feel self-hatred. Of course, he said that smiling, but it's a pretty harsh judgment. And it's also true, I noticed, in Thailand. Perhaps not so much any more: As modern culture moves in, it really does teach people to hate themselves, to feel bad about themselves. It holds up all sorts of images of physical and financial perfection that nobody can live up to. But in traditional culture, one of the basic skills of being a human being was, essentially, how to feel good about yourself, how to love yourself, how to wish yourself well, and how to act intelligently on that wish. Only really stupid people would hate themselves, and yet that kind of stupidity is rampant now in the modern world. Be careful not to pick it up.

The mind has the potential for all kinds of moods. Sometimes simply sitting and taking stock of things for a few minutes, learning how to use our powers of thought—not to destroy ourselves as many of us do, but as an assistance to the meditation—can make all the difference. We often think that to meditate is to stop thinking. Well, you have to learn how to think properly before your thoughts can stop in a skillful way.

If you're thinking in ways that are self-destructive, in ways that are really harmful to yourself, and you simply stop, it's like running a truck into a wall. You can get thrown through the windshield or suffer whiplash. But if you learn how to think in ways that are for your own true benefit—like the things we chant about every evening, which are always beneficial to think about—then when the time comes for the mind to settle down and think less and less and less and get more and more absorbed in the present moment, it's a lot easier. There's a natural deceleration.

So the way you prepare yourself to meditate, the attitudes you bring to the meditation, are very important. This doesn't mean that you should meditate only when you're in a good mood. If you're in a bad mood, think in ways that will improve your mood, that will improve your attitude toward the meditation, your attitude toward the object that you're going to be focusing on. Remind yourself that the breath is your friend, and you're here to develop the friendship even further. In that way your thinking, instead of being a distraction, is actually a component part of the meditation. It's an important step that can't be overlooked.

The Story-telling Mind

June, 2001

We've all read how the practice of meditation can dismantle our sense of self as we take a good hard look at the things we identify as *me* or *mine*. When you meditate you're supposed to come into the present moment and drop all reference to the future or the past and simply look at things as they arise. But some futures and pasts are easier to drop than others. Even if you can drop them for the time you're in meditation, you've got to come back and live with them when you come out of meditation.

This whole issue of the narratives of our lives, the stories we tell ourselves: If we could just drop them and be done with them, life would be awfully easy. Meditation would be easy. But some narratives are stickier than others. We know that the Buddha's teachings involve learning to drop a lot of things, but in some cases, before you can drop them, you have to learn how to do them skillfully. The stories you tell yourself about your life are among the things you have to learn how to do skillfully. Otherwise, you can come out of a nice, peaceful meditation, and meet up with the same old rotten story all over again. You'll find yourself relating to it and getting tied up in it again and again and again. Or else you find that you can't even get into the meditation to begin with, because no matter how hard you try to drop the story it stays stuck to your hand.

So a good part of the meditation is often not just being with the breath but—if you find you've got a story that keeps obsessing the mind, stirring up greed, anger, delusion, fear, whatever—learning how to deal with that story, learning how to tell yourself new stories. Learn a corrective to the old stories. One of the basic ways of doing this is to reflect on the passage we chanted just now, developing thoughts of goodwill, compassion, appreciation, and equanimity. Try to develop these attitudes with respect to those stories so that you can tell yourself new stories that are easier to let go of in a liberating way.

In other words, you don't just push the stories away. You weave a new story and then you get to the point in the story where it's time to settle down and meditate. That way the story will leave you alone. When you come back out of meditation, the story may still be there but it's not the kind of story that's going to get you all worked up. It's been refashioned.

Learn to get more and more skillful at the way you tell stories in the mind, starting out with an attitude of goodwill. First, good-will for yourself. You realize that if you sit here telling yourself bad stories over and over again, you're going to suffer. Do you want to suffer? Well, no. Do you want other people to suffer? Well, maybe. You may think about people who've wronged you, and of how much you'd like to see them get their just desserts. In cases like this, you have to ask yourself what you're going to gain from their suffering. You don't benefit in any way from their suffering. The fact that you're sitting here wishing suffering on them is harming *you* right now, getting in the way of your meditation.

So what you want is a story for yourself that ends up with your being happy and their being happy. That's your wish. That's the basic foundation for all the rest of the sublime attitudes.

Now in some cases you see where people are actually harming themselves, harming you, harming others. That's where you need compassion. Think about it. You really wish they could stop. And of course the same thing applies to you. When you're harming yourself, you wish you could stop causing that harm. "It would be good for that harm not to happen. It would be good for those people not to suffer." Remind yourself of that attitude.

For appreciation, you remind yourself of your goodness, of the goodness of other people, the things you've done that make you deserve to be happy, the things that other people have done that make them deserve to be happy. You're not jealous or resentful of their happiness and you don't downplay their good points.

Finally, equanimity, when you realize that some things are simply beyond your control: No matter how much goodwill you feel for other people, no matter how much appreciation and compassion you feel, some things lie totally beyond what you can change. Number one, the past cannot be changed. You have to develop equanimity toward the past. Look at what the Buddha has you think about to develop equanimity: the principle of kamma. Old kamma is old kamma and cannot be undone. What's important is your new kamma, what you're doing right now. Now, that can effect some things, but there are other things beyond the power of new kamma, largely through the continuance of old kamma. You've got to think about that and learn how to develop equanimity in cases where equanimity is appropriate.

The Buddha isn't saying that equanimity is better than the other three attitudes. You just learn which situations require which attitude: which situations require goodwill, which require compassion, which require appreciation, which require equanimity. In this way, equanimity is not simply passive acceptance. It's an ordering of your priorities, telling you to stop wasting energy on things that can't be changed, and to focus it instead on areas where good will, compassion, and appreciation can make a difference.

So you look at the stories you're telling yourself and try to inject them with these attitudes, and especially the teaching on kamma. There's no wrong that goes unpunished, no good that goes unrewarded. That's simply the way kamma is. Therefore, we don't have to carry around ledger sheets—which person did this, which person did that—with the fear that if the ledger sheet disappears then that person's not going to get the retribution he or she deserves. The principle of kamma takes care of that. But remember that it also takes care of you as well.

When you look at the satisfaction you get out of unskillful story-telling, you realize that it's pretty miserable. It's nothing you really want. It's nothing that stands up to any real scrutiny. When you see this, you find it easier to let go. You've got these other attitudes that will bring you into the present moment in a way that allows you to feel good about yourself. You're not allowing yourself to be victimized. At the same time you're not wishing ill on anybody. You do what can be done given the situation. And when the time comes where the mind needs a rest, the mind needs to settle down, that's what should be done right now. That's the best thing you can do right now. And that way the narrative leads you into the present moment.

You want to look at the attitudes you're fostering in your mind and make sure they're skillful ones—because the whole issue of kamma boils down to this: What you do right now is important. What was done in the past may have some influence on what you can do right now, but what you do right now is what's really important. And the possibility of doing something skillful right now is always present. When bad things come, you accept them as the results of past kamma, but if you realize you're doing bad kamma in the present as well, that's something you can't have equanimity for. You've got to change it. You can do your best in whatever the situation is, confident that it will work out—that if you keep on doing and saying and thinking skillful things, the results will have to be good.

So no matter how bad the situation, your hope lies in what you're doing right now. And the more you think about this, the more it brings the mind into the present moment. That's when it's ready to meditate.

If you look in the texts where the Buddha talks about the past, some of them go back many aeons, many cycles of the universe, describing how this happened, how that happened, where this came from, where that came from: long stories about past lives or cycles of lives. But these texts all end up by pointing to the basic principle that has shaped these things and is going to shape the future: the principle of kamma. And where's kamma being made? Right here, right now. So focus right here.

The same with all the cosmologies. When the Buddha describes the levels of being, the discussion comes down to where these levels of being come from. They come from the mind, from what the mind is doing in the present. Right here, right now.

Whatever the narratives are, when you tell them skillfully they bring you back to the present moment. So learn how to be a good storyteller, telling yourself the right stories, stories that will bring you into the present with a sense of confidence in your own abilities, with a sense of wellbeing, a sense of the importance of stilling the mind. No matter what the stories are—no matter what other people have done, no matter what you've done—there's a way of looking at them that can put the mind at rest. To try to find that way: This is what all the teachings on kamma, all the teachings on the sublime attitudes, are about. You weave new stories in the mind, stories in which you have a change of heart, new stories that come together right here, enabling you to stay right here with a sense of wellbeing, clarity, concentration, mindfulness, and discernment. Without anything tugging you back into the past, pulling you into the future, you're able to just be right here, right now, aware right here, right now, healing the mind right here, right now.

That's how you use the mind's storytelling ability to bring it to a point where it can just stop telling stories and look at what you've got. Learn to be skillful with what you've got right here, right now.

That's what the Buddha's teachings all come down to, this principle of skillfulness. How skillfully can you relate to the different things going on in your mind, for your own wellbeing, for the wellbeing of others around you? Meditation doesn't mean that you're cutting off any mental faculties. The mind has to tell stories. Even arahants can tell stories, can reflect on the past and plan for the future. They've simply learned to do it in a way that doesn't cause any suffering. And it's not just from their bringing the mind into the present moment. It also comes from reflecting on things in a certain way, using the Buddha's teachings as proper tools to weave skillful narratives. Let all the ways that the mind relates to itself in terms of past, future, narratives, stories, worldviews, cosmologies—all your views—become skillful. Let them no longer be a cause for suffering.

Think of the practice as an all-around way of training the mind. You're not here just to get very skillful at noting or at being with the breath. You want the mind to become very skillful in all its activities. Ajaan Fuang once said to me, when I went back to reordain, that being a meditator requires being skillful in everything, not just sitting here with your eyes closed.

You approach everything as an interesting challenge: "What's the most skillful way of dealing with this? What's the most skillful way of dealing with that?" When you have that attitude, when you've developed it and trained it in your daily life, then when you come to the meditation, things go a lot easier.

How to Fall

December, 2002

A frequent question is: How can you tell if you're making progress in your meditation? And one of the answers is: When the mind slips off its object, you get faster and faster at bringing it back. Notice, the answer isn't: The mind doesn't slip off at all. It's: You're expected to slip off; it's a normal part of the practice, a normal part of the training. The point lies in being more alert to what's going on and quicker to remedy the situation when you've slipped off the breath.

So an important part of learning how to meditate is learning how to fall. They say that when you start learning Aikido, the first thing they teach is how to fall without hurting yourself. The purpose is that it makes you less and less afraid to fall, less and less damaged, of course, by the fall, and also less likely to fall, more willing to take chances.

So the trick when you meditate is learning how to bring the mind back with a minimum amount of recrimination, a minimum amount of self-criticism, with just the simple observation, "I haven't come here to think about next week's schedule or last night's fiascoes or whatever. I'm here to focus on the breath." Simply leave those other things and come back. Learn how to do it without tying your mind up in knots.

In our modern educational system, we're quickly channeled into the activities where we have a natural talent. As a result we don't learn how to become good at things that *don't* come easily. So when we make an effort at something that doesn't come naturally, the easiest thing in the world seems to be to slip and fall and then just go with the fall and plop down, fallen. That's called *not* knowing how to fall.

The trick, when you fall, is to notice that there is a certain amount of momentum, but you don't have to give in to the momentum.

You can notice this when you've made a vow to give up something for a particular period of time. Last summer it was popular here at the monastery to give up chocolate in the evening. But then came the temptation: "What's wrong with a little bit of chocolate?" Well, there's nothing really wrong with chocolate *per se,* so it was easy to rationalize and come to the decision to drop the vow, to go for the chocolate. The problem, of course, is that the important part of the vow wasn't the chocolate, it was the training in sticking to your vow no matter what. All too often we assume that once that decision to drop a vow has been made, it can't be unmade; you're powerless and have to follow through with the momentum. But it *is* possible to unmake that decision—in the next moment or two moments later, three moments later. This is called learning how to fall properly. In other words, you don't give in to the momentum that leads you away. You realize that you're always free to change your mind immediately and come back.

When you notice yourself slipping off the breath, don't just give in to the momentum of having slipped. Catch yourself: "I can just turn around," and you'll be amazed at how quickly you *can* turn around. Now, the mind may come up with other reasons: "Oh no, you can't turn around now; you've committed yourself." Well, that's interesting! You've suddenly committed yourself to the distraction—which isn't committed to you—and you don't feel you've committed yourself to your meditation. This is one of the many tricks the mind plays on itself. The important point is learning how to see through those tricks, not to believe them, and to have a few tricks of you own.

There's a part of the mind that says it's a lot more natural to take the easy way out, but that begs the question of nature versus nurture. If you go to a psychotherapist, you learn very clearly how your particular habits got developed by a particular way your parents raised you or by particular experiences you had when you were a kid. That means those habits are not necessarily natural. They were learned. They're there, they're ingrained, but you can unlearn them. You can nurture the mind in the other direction, which is what we're doing as we train it in meditation. We're re-educating the mind.

And not only are we teaching it how to stay on one topic as we stay with the breath, but we're also teaching it how to come back to the breath more quickly: how to catch yourself as the mind begins to let go of the breath and latch on to something else, and to just turn right around, without any problem at all, and latch back onto the breath. This way you learn to discipline yourself without the harshness that we usually associate with the word "discipline." We're learning a more matter-of-fact way of dealing with our own mind.

You find that this cuts through a lot of the garbage. And as a result, there are fewer hooks for your defilements to hang on to. Instead of dealing with abstractions such as "my personality," "my character," "the way I am," just keep focused on the present moment. Whatever decision was made, it was made in total freedom, and if you see it's a bad decision, you have total freedom to make another decision. When you clear away your self-image—which is another hiding ground for all kinds of defilements—the playing field is a lot clearer, and there are a lot fewer places for the defilements to hide.

A woman I know in Laguna Beach once went to a meditation retreat where she was taught to bring meditation practice into daily life by viewing daily life as an interplay between the absolute and the relative. Those are pretty big abstractions, about as big as you can get. And after trying to think in these terms for a week, she came to the Sunday sitting group with a very convoluted question about how to manage her life in those terms. I must admit the question was so convoluted that I couldn't follow it, but the problem was obvious: The more abstract the abstraction, the more difficult it is to see your way clearly in the path, and the easier it is to get tied up in knots. We tend to think of abstractions as being clean and neat and Mondrian, but actually they leave room for lots of convolutions. They place lots of veils over what's really happening. When you clear away the abstractions, you have the mind right here with the breath. It can decide to stay with the breath or it can decide to move away. It's as simple as that.

The same principle applies throughout the practice. Once you've made up your mind to stick with the precepts, you keep deciding with every moment whether you're going to stick with that vow. Once you've made up your mind to stick with the breath, you keep deciding with every moment whether you're going to stick with that intention. And the more you keep things on simple terms, basic terms, down-to-earth, no-nonsense, straight-talking terms in the mind—without bringing in issues about your past, without bringing in issues about your self-image to complicate matters—you find it's a lot easier to stay on the path. It's a lot easier to bring yourself back when you fall off, because there are fewer convolutions in the terrain you're falling on. So not only when you're meditating, but also when you're practicing every aspect of the path, try to keep things as simple as possible, as down-to-earth, moment-to-moment as possible.

When I was staying with Ajaan Fuang he would sometimes ask me to do things like, "Tonight sit up and meditate all night long." "Omigosh," I responded the first time he said that, "I can't do that; I didn't get enough sleep last night and had a long, tiring day." And so on. And he said, "Is it going to kill you?" "Well, no." "Then you can do it."

As simple as that. Of course, it wasn't easy, but it was simple. And when you keep things simple, they eventually do become easier. You just stay with that moment-to-moment decision, not thinking about, "All night, all night, I've got to keep this up all night." You just think about, "This breath, this breath, this breath." Find ways to keep yourself interested in each breath as it comes, and you'll make it to morning.

That's how you bring the meditation into daily life: Keep things simple, strip them down. Once things are stripped down in the mind, the defilements don't have many places to hide. And when you do fall, you fall in a place that's easier to get up from. You don't have to give in to the momentum of the fall or get stuck in a quagmire. You catch yourself and regain your balance right away.

My mother once said that the event that first attracted her to my father happened during a meal at her home. My uncle, her brother, had invited my dad home from college for a visit. Then one day, during a meal, my dad knocked a glass of milk off the table but he caught the glass before it hit the floor. And that's why my mother married him. I know it sounds kind of crazy—I owe my existence to my father's quick reflexes—but it says something very interesting. And it's the kind of quality you want as a meditator: If you knock yourself over, well, you can pick yourself right back up. If you can do it before you hit the floor, so much the better. But even when you're flat on the floor, you're not a glass. You haven't shattered. You can still pick yourself up.

Try to keep it as simple as that.

Tuning-in to the Breath

December, 2002

When I first went to stay with Ajaan Fuang, one of the questions I asked him was, "What do you need to believe in order to meditate?" He answered that there was only one thing: the principle of kamma. Now when we hear the word "kamma," we usually think, "kamma-and-rebirth," but he meant specifically the principle of action: that what you do shapes your experience.

If you're convinced of this, you can do the meditation because, after all, the meditation is a *doing*. You're not just sitting here, biding your time, waiting for the accident of Awakening to happen. Even in very still states of meditation, there's an activity going on. Even the act of "being the knowing" is still a doing. It's a fabrication, a *sankhara*. In one of the suttas, the Buddha says that all the different *khandhas*, all the different aggregates that make up experience as a whole, have to get shaped into aggregates by the process of fabrication. In other words, there's a potential for a form, a potential for a feeling, potential for perception, fabrication, consciousness; and the act of fabricating is what turns these potentials into actual aggregates.

It sounds abstract, but it's a very important lesson for the meditation even from the very beginning. You sit here in the body—and of course, that's a fabrication right there: the idea that you're sitting in the body—but given all the many different things you could focus on right now, there's the possibility of choice. This possibility of choice is where kamma comes in. You can choose any of the sensations that are coming into your awareness. It's as if there were a buzz in all the different parts of the body. There's a potential for pain here, a potential for pleasure over there. All these different sensations are presenting themselves to you for you to do something about them, and you have the choice as to which ones you'll notice.

Doctors have done studies showing that pain isn't just a physical phenomenon. It isn't totally a given. There are so many different messages coming into your brain right now that you can't possibly process them all, so you choose to focus on just some of them. And the mind has a tendency to focus on pain because it's usually a warning signal. But we don't have to focus there. In other words, there can be a slight discomfort in a part of the body, and you can focus on it and make it more and more intense, more and more of an issue. That's *one* thing you can do right now, but—even if you may not realize it—you have the choice of whether or not to do that. You can choose *not* to make it more intense. You can choose even to ignore it entirely. Many times we have habitual ways of relating to sensations, and they're so habitual and so consistent that we think there's no choice at all. "This is the way things have to be," we think, but they don't.

That's the other implication of the principle of kamma: You can change your actions. If some parts of experience are dependent on choice and fabrication, you can choose to change. You see this really clearly when you focus on the breath. The breath is always there in the body, and if you look carefully you'll discover that it has many levels. It's like looking up in the sky: Sometimes you feel a breeze coming from the south, but you look up in the sky and see a layer of clouds moving east, and another higher layer of clouds moving west. There are lots of different layers of wind in the atmosphere and, in the same way, there are lots of different layers of breath in the body. You can choose which ones to focus on.

It's like having a radio receiver: You can choose to tune-in to different stations. The radio waves from all the nearby radio stations, all the different frequencies, are all in the air around us. There are radio waves from Los Angeles, radio waves from San Diego, even short wave radio waves from who-knows-where, all over the place. They're going through this room right now. They're going through your body right now. And when you turn on the radio you choose which frequency you want to focus on, which one you want to listen to. The same with the body. You sort out, of all the possible sensations, just one type of sensation to focus on: the breath-ness of the breath. Wherever you feel the sensation of the in-and-out breath most clearly, you focus right there. Now some of us have a radio we haven't taken very good care of, and as soon as we tune it in to one station it slips over to another. So you've got to keep tuning it back, tuning it back.

But the problem isn't just the tuning. It's what you do with the sensation once you've tuned-in to it. Again, you can focus on the breath in a way that makes it painful, or you can focus on it in a way that makes it comfortable. You're not faced just with the given-ness of the breath. What you do with it can make it more or less painful, more or less comfortable. To continue the analogy, it's like having a volume control on the radio: You can turn it way up loud so that it hurts your ears, or you can turn it way down soft so that you can hardly hear it at all. But as you get more skillful with your volume control, you get a sense of what's just right so that you can adjust the level and the pressure of your focus for maximum enjoyment.

As you get tuned-in more and more precisely, you discover there are other subtleties as well. Again, like the radio, when you really get tuned very precisely onto the frequency, the static goes away and you can hear subtleties in the signal that you couldn't hear before. You can play with them, turn up the treble, turn up the base, whatever you want. So even though the radio signal is a given, you can do a lot with it. That's the element of kamma in your meditation right now: It's what you're doing with the breath.

You can learn how to be more skillful in how you relate to it so that you can sense not only the very obvious breath of the air coming in and out of the lungs, but also the sensations that go through the whole body as you breathe in, as you breathe out, the patterns of movement in the body that actually bring the air into the lungs and let it go out. There's a wave going through the body each time you breathe. As you become sensitive to it, you begin to sense where there's tension in the body, and where there's not; where the subtle breath flows properly, and where it doesn't.

And, again, it's not just a given. You can do things with that flow. You can improve the flow. If you notice tension in a certain part of the body, you relax it; and oftentimes doing this improves the breath flow not only at that one spot but also in other parts of the body as well. You begin to have a sense of the body as a whole series of different interconnected energy patterns. A tightening up here may lead to a tightening up over there, and it all gets connected in a feeling of overall constriction, of bands of tension squeezing the body. Or you can loosen it up. That's your choice. You can relax this bit of tension here and find that it leads to an unraveling of tension over there. Or you might find that everything gets so loose that you drift off. This means that you've got to learn how to gain a sense of "just right" so that you can stay with the sensation, keep your focus, and even if the radio signal begins to drift a little bit, you can follow it precisely and stay right with it.

At this point you can let go of the sensation of the in-and-out breath—the coarse breath, the obvious breath—and focus more on the subtle breath flow in the body. As you work through all the different parts of the body where it feels tense or blocked or sort of squeezed out, you let the breath sensations fill all those little nooks and crannies, and there comes a greater and greater sense of fullness, refreshment. That's what *piti* means. It's the drinking-in of the good sensation. We normally translate *piti* as rapture, but it's also related to the word for drinking, *pivati*. You drink-in this nice sensation. It feels full, it feels refreshing all the way through the body because you've opened up all the little cells in the body and allowed the breath to enter. When you get that sense of fullness, it's easier to relax.

This may not be a pretty image, but the mind at this point is like a mosquito when it's finally hit a big vein in your body. It sticks its little proboscis in and just stays right there, bathed in bliss. Its wings go weak, its feet go weak, and no matter how much you try to brush it away, it just doesn't want to go. It's just drinking-in what it wants. The same with the mind: As soon as that refreshing breath sensation begins to fill the body, you let go of everything else. No matter what other disturbances come, you're not the least bit interested because you've got something really satisfying. You could almost say that it's a sensation to die for. You let down your guard, let go of everything else, because this sensation is so totally absorbing. You've opened up every part of the body, every part of your awareness for this sensation to come in.

As you stay there and the mind grows more and more still, you become aware of a deeper sensation of absolute fullness with no sense of flowing back and forth—a real stillness in the body. There's a slight sense of air exchange on the very surface of the body, the surface of your awareness, but deep down inside there's a great stillness. There's no longer the sense of drinking-in because you're absolutely full. Ajaan Lee uses the image of an ice cube: A vapor's coming off the cube—a very vaporous movement around the edge of your awareness—but everything else is solid and still.

And then finally even the vapor stops, and the solidity fills your entire awareness. It's accompanied by a sense of brightness, even though you may not sense this brightness as a light. It's a peculiar quality: a physical sensation, a feeling tone, of brightness, clarity, radiance, filling the whole body, and you're just sitting there in the middle of it.

There's no need to rush through these stages, no need to go jumping through hoops. In fact, it's best that you *not* try to rush. Just find one sensation you can tuned-in to. Stay right there and it will develop on its own, simply because of the consistency of your focus. When you finally reach that sense of solid stillness and stay there, you begin to realize that you can choose to give a shape to it or not. You can focus on the sensations that give you a sense of the shape of the body or you can choose to ignore them. This is where you really see the principle of kamma coming into play in the meditation. It's almost as if the various sensations of the body have turned into a mist. There are these little breath droplets just shimmering there, and you sense the space in between them. The whole body is filled with this space, which also extends outside the body in every direction. Instead of focusing on the little droplets, you can focus on the space. This gives you a really clear lesson in how much choice you have in how you experience the present moment. Just the simple sensation of having a body here comes from sub-conscious shape-giving choices you've made. You realize there are lots of different sensations you can focus on, and there's a skill in how you choose your sensations, in how you magnify the ones you want, and how you just put aside the ones you don't.

So even though this is just training in concentration, there's also a lot of discernment involved. As the Buddha once said, both tranquility and insight are required for getting good strong states of absorption. And he never talked about insight without framing it in terms of kamma, in terms of the skillfulness of what you're doing.

So this practice is what lays the groundwork so that—when the time comes to consider issues of inconstancy, stress, and not-self—you've got the proper context. You've created a good space inside, a good space in the present moment, so that there's no hungry sense of having to grasp after this or grasp after that. When you've drunk your fill of the fullness and stillness, you're in a much better mood to consider things for what they actually are—so that when insight comes it's not destabilizing. Without this solid foundation, thinking about inconstancy, stress, or not-self can get really disorienting. But when you start thinking about these issues in the context of what you're doing in the meditation, they make it even more stabilizing. This is where concentration, tranquility, insight, and discernment all come together in a healthy and balanced way.

Bathed in the Breath

December, 2002

When there's a Dhamma talk, you don't have to listen. The important thing is to stay with your breath. When the breath comes in, you know it's coming in; when it goes out, you know it's going out. Try to make that experience of the breath fill your awareness as much as possible. The Dhamma talk here is a fence to keep you corralled with the breath. When the mind wanders off, here's the sound of the Dhamma to remind you to go back to the breath, but when you're with the breath you don't need reminding. You do your own reminding. That's what the mindfulness does in the meditation. Each time you breathe in, each time you breathe out, remind yourself to stay with the breath. Make just a little mental note: "This is where you want to stay, this is where you want to stay."

And try not to think of yourself as inhabiting one part of the body watching the breath in another part of the body. Think of the breath as all around you. It's coming in and out the front, coming in and out the back, down from the top, all the way out to your fingers, all the way out to your toes. There's a subtle breath energy coming in and out of the body all the time. If you're in one part of the body watching the breath in the other part, you're probably blocking the breath energy to make space for that sense of "you" in the part of the body that's watching. So think of yourself as totally surrounded by the breath, bathed in the breath, and then survey the whole body to see where there are still sections of the body that are tense or tight, that are preventing the breath from coming in and going out. Allow them to loosen up.

This way you allow for the fullness of the breath to come in, go out, each time there's an in-breath, each time there's an out-breath.

Actually the fullness doesn't go in and out. There's just a quality of fullness that's bathed by the breath coming in, bathed by the breath going out. It's not squeezed out by the breath. It's not forced out by the breath. Each nerve in the body is allowed to relax and have a sense of fullness, right here, right now. Simply try to maintain that sense of fullness by the way you breathe. Your focus is on the breath, but you can't help but notice the fullness.

If you can't get that sense of fullness going throughout the whole body, find at least some part of the body that doesn't feel squeezed out, that feels open and expansive, and then see if you can copy that same feeling tone in other parts of the body. Notice the other different parts of the body where it feels open like that and allow them to connect. At first, nothing much will happen from that sense of connection, but allow it to stay open, stay open. Each time you breathe in, each time you breathe out, maintain that sense of openness, openness, and the sense of connection will get stronger.

This is why the ability to stay with these sensations is so important, for your staying with them is what allows them to grow. If you move off to someplace else, if you're thinking of something else, there will have to be a tensing-up in the body to allow that thought to happen. Whatever sense of fullness might have developed—say, in your arms or your legs, in different parts of the body, down your back—doesn't have a chance to develop. It gets squeezed off because you're not paying attention to it any more.

This is why the Buddha talks about concentration as *mahaggatam cittam:* an enlarged awareness. If your awareness is limited just to one little spot, everything else gets squeezed out, everything else gets blotted out—and what is that if not ignorance? You're trying to make your awareness 360 degrees, all around in all directions, because the habit of the mind is to focus its awareness in one spot here, then one spot there, moving around, but there's always the one spot, one spot, one spot. It opens up a little bit and then squeezes off again, opens up a little bit, squeezes off again, and nothing has a chance to grow. But if you allow things to open up throughout the *whole* body, you realize that if you think about anything at all you destroy that openness. So you've got to be very, very careful, very, very still, to allow this open fullness to develop.

So these qualities of consistency, care, and heedfulness are important in allowing this state of concentration to develop. Without them, nothing much seems to happen. You have a little bit of concentration, then you step on it, a little bit of concentration, then you squeeze it off as you go looking at something else, thinking about something else. And so whatever little bits and pieces of concentration you do have, don't seem very remarkable. They don't get a chance to be remarkable. Concentration takes time—and our society's pretty extraordinary in fostering the expectation that things should happen quickly. If anything's going to be good, it has to happen quickly, it has to be instant. And so, by and large, we've lost the ability to stay with things as they develop slowly. We've lost the ability to keep chipping away, chipping away, chipping away at a large task that's going to take time and can't be speeded up.

When the Buddha gives images for practicing concentration, he often relates them to skills. Skills take time, and he was teaching people who had taken the time to master many useful skills. In Thailand, they still sharpen knives against stones, and it's a skill you have to learn: how not to ruin the knife as you're sharpening it. If you get impatient and try to speed things up, you'll ruin the sharpness, the straightness of the blade. So you have to be very still. The mind has to be still, and you have to maintain just the right amount of pressure constantly as you sharpen the blade. At first it may seem like nothing is happening, but over time the blade does get sharper and sharper. The consistency of your pressure is what guarantees that the blade won't get worn in one particular spot— too sharp in one spot and not sharp enough in another, too sharp in the sense that the blade is no longer straight. You've worn it down too much in one spot. There are a lot of things you have to watch out for, simply in the act of sharpening a blade. But if you have that skill in your repertoire, then when the time comes to meditate, it's easier to relate to what you're doing: that same kind of consistency, that same evenness of pressure, the continual mindfulness and alertness that are needed to maintain the proper pressure.

Another skill sometimes used as an analogy is that of a hunter. A hunter has to be very quiet so as not to scare the animals off, and at the same time very alert so as not to miss when a particular animal comes by. In the same way, we as meditators have to be careful not to slip off in either direction: into too much stillness or too much mental activity. You have to find the proper balance. I was once talking to an anthropologist who said that of all the skills in primitive societies that anthropologists try to learn, the hardest is hunting. It requires the strongest concentration, the most sensitivity. So here we're not hunting animals, but we're hunting concentration, which is even more subtle and requires even more stillness and alertness.

Sometimes we in the West think that we come to the Dhamma with an advantage: We've got so much education, we're so well-read. But we have a major disadvantage in that we lack the patience and consistency that come with mastering a skill. So keep that in mind as you're meditating, when you find yourself getting impatient for results. You have to be watchful and consistent. You need that sense of being bathed by the breath, being open to the breathing sensations in all parts of the body down to every little pore of your skin. Then you learn the sensitivity that's required, the consistency that's required, to maintain that. That way the sense of fullness can grow and grow and grow until it becomes really gratifying, really satisfying, to give your concentration the kind of strength, the sense of refreshment, the sense of nourishment it needs in order to keep going.

Ajaan Fuang once said that without this sense of fullness, refreshment, or rapture, your meditation gets dry. You need this lubricant to keep things smooth and running: the sense of well-being and refreshment, the immediate visceral pleasure of being in a concentrated state.

At the same time, it heals all our mental wounds: any sense of tiredness, of being stressed-out, mistreated, abused. It's like medicine for these mental wounds. Now, medicine often takes time to work, especially *soothing* and *reconstituting* medicine. Think of the creams you put on chapped skin. The skin isn't immediately cured when you first rub on the cream. It takes time. The skin has to be exposed to the cream for long periods of time to allow the cream to do its work. The same with concentration. It's a treatment that takes time. Your nervous system needs to be exposed to the sense of fullness for a long period of time, giving it a chance to breathe in, breath out all around so that the mindfulness and the breath together can do their healing work.

So don't get impatient. Don't feel that nothing is happening. A lot of things that are very important require time, and they do their work subtly. If you give them the time they need, you find that you're more than repaid. After all, you could be sitting for the whole hour planning next week, planning next month, planning next year. What will you have at the end of the hour? A lot of plans. And part of you may feel satisfied that you've provided for the future, but when you reflect on how many of your past plans have actually borne results, you'll realize the odds against your new plans' ever amounting to much. What would you have to show for your hour then? Nothing very certain. Maybe nothing but mouse-droppings and straw. But if you give the breath an hour to do its healing work, totally opening up the body to allow the breath to bathe every nerve out to every pore, you know that you'll come out at the end of the hour with a body and mind in much better shape. The body will be soothed; the mind, bright and alert.

And you don't need to stop being bathed in the breath when the hour is up. You can keep it going in all your activities. That way, even though you may not be armed with a whole set of plans for facing the future, at least you're in a position where you don't need that kind of armor. You've got the armor of a healthy body and mind. You've got an invisible armor: the force-field of this all-encompassing breath, continually streaming out from your center to every pore, protecting you on all sides. That's something you feel in every cell of your body, something you know for sure, for you can sense it all around you, right here, right now. And you know that whatever the future brings, you're prepared. You can handle it.

This sense of fullness, brightness, alertness: That's all you'll need to keep the mind capable, healthy, and strong.

The Steps of Breath Meditation

November, 2002

When the Buddha teaches breath meditation, he teaches sixteen steps in all. They're the most detailed meditation instructions in the Canon. And the breath is the topic he recommends most highly, most frequently—because the breath is not only a place where the mind can settle down and gain concentration, but it's also something the mind can analyze. It's where all the insights needed for Awakening can arise—while the mind is being mindful of the breath, alert to the breath, and also conscious of how it relates to the breath.

In the later stages of breath meditation the emphasis is focused less on the breath than on the mind as it relates to the breath. In the beginning stages, though, the emphasis is on the breath itself, on using the breath to snare the mind and bring it into the present moment. In the first two steps you're simply with long breathing and short breathing, sensitizing yourself to what long and short breathing feel like. Beginning with the third step, though, there's an element of volition. You train yourself, and the first thing you train yourself to do is to be aware of the whole body as you breathe in, aware of the whole body as you breathe out.

When the Buddha describes concentration states, he doesn't use images of single-pointedness. He uses images of whole-body awareness. When a sense of rapture and pleasure comes from the breath, he tells you to knead that sense of rapture and pleasure through the whole body, the way you would knead water into flour to make dough. Another image is of the rapture welling up from within the body and filling the body just like a spring of cool water coming up from within a lake, filling the entire lake with its coolness. Another image is of lotuses standing in a lake: Some of the lotuses don't go above the water but stay totally immersed in the water, saturated from their roots to their tips with the stillness and coolness of the water in the lake. Still another image is of a person wrapped in white cloth, totally surrounded by the white cloth from head to foot, so that all of his body is covered by the white cloth.

These are all images of whole-body awareness, of a sense of rapture, pleasure, or bright awareness filling the entire body. That's what you want to work on when you get to know the breath, because the type of awareness that allows insight to arise is not restricted to one point. When you're focused on one point and blot out everything else, that leaves a lot of blind spots in the mind. But when you try to get a more all-around awareness, it helps eliminate the blind spots. In other words, you want to be immersed in the breath, aware of the breath all around you.

One of the phrases they use for this—*kayagatasati*—is mindfulness immersed in the body. The body is saturated with awareness, and the awareness itself gets immersed in the body, is surrounded by the body. So it's not that you're up in one spot—say, in the back of the head—looking at the rest of the body from that one spot, or trying to block awareness of the rest of the body from that one spot of awareness. You've got to have a whole-body awareness, all-around, 360 degrees, so as to eliminate the blind spots in the mind.

Once you have this type of awareness, you work at maintaining it—although the "work" here is not like other work. You work at not moving your attention, at not letting it shrink. You work at not taking on other responsibilities. With time, though, the work becomes more natural, more second-nature. You feel more and more settled and at home. As the mind settles in, its usual nervous energy begins to dissolve. The body actually needs less and less oxygen, because the level of your brain activity begins to grow calm, and so the breath gets more and more refined. It can even grow perfectly still, for all the oxygen you need is coming in through the pores of your skin.

At this point the breath and your awareness seem to have melted into each other. It's hard to draw a line between the two and, for the time being, you don't try. Allow the awareness and the breath to interpenetrate, to become one.

You have to allow this awareness, this sense of oneness, to get really solid. Otherwise it's easily destroyed because the tendency of the mind is to shrink up. As soon as we think, we shrink up the energy field in certain parts of the body to block them out of our awareness, which is why there's tension in the body every time a thought occurs. This part of the body gets tense so you can think that thought; that part of the body gets tense so you can think this one, back and forth this way. It's no wonder that the simple process of thinking takes a lot out of the body. According to some Chinese medical treatises, a person whose work is mental tends to use up energy at three times the rate of a person whose work is totally physical. This is because thinking involves tension in the body. And, in particular, thoughts that go off into the past or into the future have to create whole worlds for themselves to inhabit.

When we're getting the mind concentrated, we're thinking in a different way. In the beginning stages we're still thinking, but we're thinking solely about the present moment, observing solely the present moment, being alert and mindful to what's going on here, so we don't have to create worlds of past and future. This imposes less stress on the body. In order to maintain that present focus and not go slipping off to your old habits, you've got to keep your awareness as broad as possible. That's what keeps you rooted in the present moment, all the way down to your fingers and toes. When your awareness stays broad, it prevents the kind of shrinking up that allows the mind to slip out after thoughts of past and future. You stay fully inhabiting the present. The need to think gets more and more attenuated.

When fewer and fewer thoughts interfere with the flow of the breath energy, a sense of fullness develops throughout the body. The text refers to this fullness as rapture, and the sense of ease accompanying it as pleasure. You let this sense of easy fullness suffuse the body, but you still maintain your focus on the breath energy, even if it's totally still. Eventually—and you don't have to rush this—the point will come when the body and mind have had enough of the rapture and ease, and you can allow them to subside. Or there may be times when the rapture gets too overpowering, in which case you try to refine your awareness of the breath so that it can come in under the radar of the rapture, and you move to a level of total ease. Then even the ease—the sense of imbibing the pleasure—subsides, leaving you with total stillness.

After you've become settled in the stillness, you can start looking for the dividing line between awareness and the breath. Up to this point you've been manipulating the breath, trying to get more and more sensitive to what feels comfortable in the breathing and what doesn't, so that your manipulation gets more and more subtle, to the point where you can drop the manipulation and just be with the breath. This allows the breath to grow more and more refined until it's absolutely still. When things are really solid, really still, your awareness and the object of your awareness naturally separate out, like chemicals in a suspension that's allowed to stay still. Once the awareness separates out, you can begin directly manipulating the factors of the mind, the feelings and perceptions that shape your awareness. You can watch them as they do this, for now the breath is out of the way.

It's like tuning-in to a radio station: As long as there's static, as long as you aren't precisely tuned-in to the station's frequency, you can't hear the subtleties of the signal. But once you're right at the frequency, the static goes away and all the subtleties become clear. When you're tuned-in to the mind, you can see the subtleties of feeling and perception as they move. You can see the results they give, the impact they have on your awareness, and after a while you get the sense that the more refined that impact, the better. So you allow them to calm down. When they're calmed down, you're left with awareness itself.

But even this awareness has its ups and downs, and to get you past them the Buddha has you manipulate them, just as you manipulated the breath and the mental factors of feeling and perception. The text talks about gladdening the mind, steadying the mind, and releasing the mind. In other words, as you get more and more used to the stages of concentration, you begin to gain a sense of which kind of concentration your awareness needs right now. If it seems unstable, what can you do to steady it? How do you change your perception of the breath or adjust your focus to make the mind more solid? When the meditation starts getting dry, what can you do to gladden the mind? And as you're moving from one stage of concentration to the next, exactly what do you let go that releases the mind from the weaker stage of concentration and allows it to settle in a stronger one?

When the Buddha talks about releasing the mind at this point in the practice, he's not talking about ultimate release. He's talking about the kind of release that occurs as you let go, say, of the directed thought and evaluation of the first jhana, releasing yourself from the burden of those factors as you move into the second jhana, and so on through the different levels of concentration. As you do this, you begin to see how much those levels of concentration are willed. This is important. Insight can come while you're in concentration as you move from one stage to the next, as you notice out of the corner of your mind's eye what you do to move from one way of experiencing the breath to the next, one level of solidity to the next. And you see how much this is a produced phenomenon.

This finally leads to the stages of breath meditation associated with insight. First there's insight into inconstancy, both in the breath, but more importantly in the mind, as you see that even these stable, very refreshing levels of concentration are willed. Underlying all the refreshment, all the stability, is a repeated willing, willing, willing to keep the state of concentration going. There's an element of burdensomeness there. Insight into inconstancy or impermanence has less to do with how you consume experiences than it does with how you produce them. You see all the effort that goes into producing a particular type of experience, and the question becomes, "Is it worth it? Isn't this burdensome, having to keep making, making, making these experiences all the time?"

Then the problem becomes, "What are you going to do to let go of this burden?" If you don't fabricate these states of concentration, is your only choice to go back to fabricating other kinds of experiences? Or is it possible not to fabricate any experience at all? All of our normal experiences from moment to moment to moment, whether in concentration or out, have an element of intention, an element of will. And now you've come to the point where that element of will, that element of intention, begins to stand out as an obvious burden. Particularly when you look around to ask, "Who am I producing this for? Exactly who is consuming this?" You come to see that your sense of who you are, who this consumer is, is difficult to pin down, because it's all made out of the aggregates, and the aggregates themselves are inconstant, stressful, and not-self. This consumer is something produced as well. This gives rise to a quality the texts call *nibbida,* which can be translated as disenchantment or disillusionment. Sometimes the translation gets stronger: revulsion. In all cases it's a sense that you've had enough of this. You feel trapped by this process. You no longer find any satisfaction here. You want to find a way out.

So you focus on letting go. According to the texts, first there's a focus on dispassion, then a focus on cessation, then finally a focus on total relinquishment. In other words, in the final stage you let go of every kind of doing, every kind of volition, of the producer, of the consumer, of the observer, even of the perceptions and the thought-fabrications that make up the path. When the path-factors have done their job you can let them go as well.

All of this takes place right at the breath, at the point where the mind and the body meet at the breath. This is why the Buddha never has you totally drop the breath as your theme of meditation. Progress along the path comes simply from staying right here and growing more and more aware of what's going on all around right here. You develop a more all-around awareness, not only all-around in the body, but also all-around in the mind. You see through the blind spots that allowed you to consume experiences obliviously, forgetting the fact that you had to produce them. It's like watching a movie—two hours of lights flashing up on a screen—and then later seeing a documentary about how they made the movie. You realize that months, sometimes years of labor went into it, and the question becomes, "Was it worth it?" A few brief hours of empty enjoyment and then you forget about it—despite all the work, all the suffering that went into making it.

So when you look at all your experiences in the same way, seeing all the effort that goes into their production and asking if it's worth it: That's when you really get disillusioned, disenchanted, when you can really let go. You let go not only of perceptions or feelings as they come and go, but also of the act of creating these things. You see that this act of creating is all-pervasive, covers all your experiences. You're always creating, either skillfully or unskillfully. There is constant production every time there's an intention, every time there's a choice in the mind. This is what begins to seem oppressive; this is what finally impels you to let go.

You let go of the producing, you let go of the creation, and the letting-go really opens things up. The mind opens to another dimension entirely: one that's not made up, not created, where there's no arising or passing away. And that too is touched right here, although at that moment there's no sense of breath, no sense of the body, no sense of the mind as a functioning, creating consumer or producer. When the Buddha talks about it, all his words are analogies, and all the analogies are of freedom. That's about all that can be said when you try to describe it, but there's a lot that can be said about how to get there. That's why the Buddha's teachings are so extensive. He goes into a lot of detail on how to get there, outlining all of the steps. But if you want to know what the goal is like, don't go looking for extensive descriptions. Just follow the steps and you'll know for yourself right here.

The Observer

August 5, 2003

Sometimes meditation is easy; sometimes it's hard. But whether it's easy or hard, we have to keep our minds on an even keel. When it gets easy, don't get complacent. If you get complacent, things start loosening up, like screws loosening up in your car. After a while things begin to rattle and then they fall off. At the same time when things don't go well, don't get upset. Rule number one in either case is to keep the mind on an even keel. Have a strong sense of the observer, the part of the mind that's simply watching what's going on, and identify as much as you can with that.

Ajaan Suwat once mentioned that when he first went to stay with Ajaan Mun his mind seemed to be all over the place. He'd sit and mediate and be thinking about this, thinking about that, and he was afraid to tell Ajaan Mun for fear of what Ajaan Mun might say. But then he realized, "I'm here to learn." So he went to see Ajaan Mun, to see what kind of advice he would give.

And Ajaan Mun's response was this: "Well, at least you're aware of what's happening. That's better than not being aware of your distractions at all." Then he quoted the Discourse on the Foundations of Mindfulness: Being aware of a scattered mind when it's scattered counts as one of the foundations of mindfulness.

Ajaan Suwat handled that lesson really well. He realized that Ajaan Mun was not praising him but simply giving him some comfort, giving him some encouragement. He wasn't saying that where he was was just fine, but he *was* reminding him that it wasn't a total disaster, that the fact that he was meditating was better than not meditating at all.

This often happens with people: Things don't go well in their meditation and they say, "Well, tonight's just not my night to meditate.

I'd do better to stop." *Not meditating is not the answer.* Even though it may not be pleasant, sitting through a bad meditation is better than not meditating. There may be some point in the course of the meditation when you finally come to your senses, when you see something in there that you didn't see before. This is why that sense of the observer is so important.

In the Canon they talk about the person who's got his or her theme of meditation well in hand, and the image they use is of a person sitting who's watching someone lying down, or of a person standing who's watching someone sitting. In other words, you place yourself a little bit above what's going on and you watch it. You step back to see what's happening from a better perspective, to get a sense of where the imbalance is in your mind, to watch what you're doing, and to think about what you might do differently.

Exactly why is the meditation going poorly? What's lacking? Ajaan Fuang once advised making a mental note of the seven factors that Ajaan Lee sets out in his Method #2, and then comparing your meditation with them, to see what's lacking. If you've got all seven component factors, then the mind is going to settle down for sure: mindful, solid, and still. So check to see what's lacking. Are you not clear about the lengths of the breaths? Are you not clear about whether the breath is comfortable? Are you not spreading the comfortable breath sensations? Do you not have a resting place for the mind, for the breath in the body? Just go down the list, and if you find that any of the component factors are missing, try to make up for the lack.

But again, to do this you need that sense of the observer, the person who's watching and doesn't get upset by what's happening, doesn't get carried away, but just watches in total neutrality. When you can watch in this way, then even a bad meditation isn't a total disaster. You take it as a challenge. Tonight's meditation may be a little bit different from last night's. Last night's went well, but you start out tonight and things don't seem to be going so well. Instead of getting flustered, just ask: "Is it a question of the body? Is something wrong with the breath? Is something wrong with your energy level? Are you too manic? Too depressed?" Lots of different factors can be playing a role here, either factors in the mind or factors in the body. If your energy level is too low, you can change the way you breathe to energize yourself. If your energy is too frenetic, you can breathe in a way that calms you down.

Try to be as precisely observant as possible. Many times what makes a difference in the meditation is the details, the little things, and if you're not paying careful attention, simply going through the motions, you miss a lot. You may be missing something important even though it seems minor. Try to go through every aspect very meticulously, try to be very observant, be *close* in your powers of observation.

There's a word in Thai, *thii,* that's used to describe the closeness, say, of the teeth in your comb or the pickets in a fence—any series of things. It's also used to describe the frequency of a radio signal. The higher the frequency the *closer* the frequency. So you want your acts of mindfulness, your acts of alertness, to be very *close:* right next to each other, with no gaps. Otherwise, if you leave a lot of gaps there's plenty of time for the curtains to come down in the mind. The backstage crew can change the scenery, and when the curtain comes up again you're off someplace else. But if your mindfulness is close like this, then they have no time to bring down the curtain. If they change the scenery you see it happening, and that destroys the illusion that otherwise would carry you away.

So whatever happens in the meditation, always stop and take stock of, "Where's the observer right now?"—in other words, the part of the mind that can simply watch and not be moved by events at all. We're so used to living in the part of the mind that's constantly pushed around by events that it almost seems traitorous to step back and be in the part that's not moved by anything at all, not touched by anything at all, that just watches, seeing what's going on. There's always that corner in the mind. So try to locate it, get familiar with it. Learn how to make that the basis of your stance, so that no matter what happens you see the events clearly for what they are. You clearly see the connection between cause and effect. That puts you in a position where you can use your ingenuity to make changes, adjust things here, adjust things there, try this, try that. Even if what you try doesn't work out, you've learned something. You've learned that that particular tactic doesn't work here, which is something worth knowing.

If you take this attitude then no matter how well the meditation goes, no matter how poorly it goes, it's always an opportunity to learn.

Judicious vs. Judgmental

May, 2003

One of the most difficult but necessary skills we need to develop as meditators is learning how to be judicious without being judgmental. And as a preliminary step to developing that skill, it's good to reflect on the difference between the two.

Being judgmental is basically an effort to get rid of something we don't understand and probably don't *want* to understand. We see something we don't like and we try to dismiss it, to stamp it out without taking the time to understand it. We're impatient. Whatever we're being judgmental about, we just want to get rid of it quickly.

Being judicious, however, requires patience together with understanding. A judicious choice is one you've made after understanding all the options, all the sides of a question. That way your choice is based on knowledge, not on greed, aversion, or delusion.

This is why the Buddha, in his analysis of the four truths, said that our task with the regard to the first truth—the truth of suffering or stress—is to comprehend it. All too often we treat pain in the same way we treat anything we don't like: We want to get rid of it as fast as possible without taking the time to understand it. So what we're learning as we practice is how not to be judgmental about the things we don't like inside ourselves. We develop the patience and the skill we need in order to stop and take a good long look at these things so that we can deal with them judiciously, so we can deal with them through understanding. We give them space so that we can watch them, can understand them, so that when we finally decide that they really are unskillful, that we really don't want to have them going on in our mind, we can get rid of them neatly, effectively.

The problem with being judgmental is that it's not effective. We try to stamp out things here and they go springing up someplace else, as in the old movie, *The Thing*. The Thing would go underground and suddenly spring up someplace else. If you cut off one head here, one identity here, its underground roots and tentacles would spring up with a new, even more horrific identity someplace else. The same thing happens when we try to get rid of anything in the mind when we don't understand its roots, don't understand where it's coming from.

Being judicious, though, is more effective. It's more precise. We see what's really skillful, what's really unskillful in the mind, and we learn how to disentangle the two. Often our skillful and unskillful habits get entangled. The things we don't like within ourselves actually do have some good in them, but we don't notice it. We focus instead on what we don't like, or what we're afraid of, and we end up trying to stamp it all out, the good along with the bad.

So this is why we meditate: to step back a bit, to watch things patiently so that we can see them for what they are and deal with them effectively. Our concentration practice gives us a comfortable center in our awareness where we can rest, where we feel less threatened by things. When we feel less threatened and less oppressed, we have the resilience to be more patient, to look into what's going on in the mind, and to develop the proper attitudes toward what is skillful and what isn't.

This is where the four sublime attitudes come in. Back in the 70's I read a book about Buddhism whose author tried to organize everything around the four noble truths but couldn't figure how the four sublime attitudes fit into the framework of the four truths. They just didn't seem to connect anyplace at all, so the author ended up treating them as an entirely separate topic. But actually the four sublime attitudes underlie the whole practice. They're the reason the Buddha focused his teaching on the four noble truths. You need a sense of goodwill to be even interested in the question of trying to understand suffering, because you want to find an effective way of dealing with it. You want to be rid of suffering, to experience wellbeing, precisely because you have goodwill for yourself and for others. So as meditators we try to use that attitude, that desire, as a way of developing the center we need in order to work toward that wellbeing from a position of strength. If you don't have that basic sense of goodwill, you'll have a hard time trying to stir up the energy needed to master the concentration, to keep with the breath, to keep coming back to the breath no matter how many times you wander off.

Now, you may want to be at a more advanced stage than trying to rein in the mind. You want to sit down and *Bung,* there it is: the first jhana. But when it doesn't happen quickly you get frustrated. So put that frustration aside. Put away all the pride and the shadow side of pride, which is the shame. Just put those things aside, and remind yourself that this is the way things are, this is where you are, and be willing just to keep coming back, coming back, to stick with those simple tasks. The people who master any kind of skill are the ones who are willing to step back and master the simple steps, to practice them over and over again, because it's in doing the simple steps and being observant that you learn many of your most important lessons.

These steps are not just a mechanical process that you have to bulldoze your way through as quickly as possible. You have to pay attention to what you're doing even when things are not going well. Pay attention to how the mind slips off, pay attention to how you bring it back, and you'll learn an awful lot right there. Underlying all this has to be an attitude of good-natured goodwill. If there's a sense of frustration, remember that you're here because of goodwill, not for the sake of frustration, not for the sake of finding some new thing to beat yourself over the head about or to be judgmental about. You're here for the sake of goodwill, for the sake of giving the mind a place where it can settle in and be at ease.

Develop compassion for yourself. Think of all the suffering you could be causing yourself if you weren't meditating. Think of all the suffering you might be causing others if you weren't meditating. This helps to remind you that when things aren't going all that well in the meditation, it's still a lot better than most of the things that people do in their lives. It's a good, beneficial use of your time.

Then develop an attitude of sympathetic joy, appreciating the
happiness you can develop through the practice, appreciating the
happiness of others. Of all the four sublime attitudes, sympathetic
joy gets the least press. It's often the hardest to develop. There
seem to be voices in our heads that resent happiness—either the
happiness of other people or, if other people have resented our
happiness, we've picked up their voices someplace and can even be
distrustful of our own happiness. So we have to counter those
voices by realizing that there is nothing wrong with happiness. It
comes through our actions. If the happiness that someone is experiencing right now doesn't seem to be deserved in terms of his or
her present actions, there must be something in the past to account
for it. At the same time, remind yourself that an attitude of resentment doesn't help you or anyone else at all. Sometimes it seems
unfair that some people are happy and others are not. But for the
time being, just put the question of fairness or unfairness aside.
Wherever there's a sense of wellbeing in the mind, learn how to
appreciate that sense of wellbeing. It has its uses.

Most people, when they experience happiness, get complacent,
which is one of the reasons why the quest for happiness is often
branded as selfish. People enjoying power or beauty or wealth tend to
get complacent and as a result of their complacency start doing very
unskillful things. But if you approach happiness from the attitude of
someone who's practicing as the Buddha taught, there is a use for
happiness. It's a quality in the mind that, if properly used, can bring
about peace of mind. After all, the concentration we're looking for in
our practice has to have some basis in wellbeing. Otherwise the mind
wouldn't be able to stay here. So if you learn how to use that sense
of wellbeing properly, without complacency, it has no drawbacks.

The Buddha, when he was practicing austerities all those years
and years in the wilderness prior to his Awakening, had a very
unhealthy attitude toward happiness. He was afraid of it. He was
afraid of pleasure, afraid that it would lead to all kinds of detrimen-
tal things in the mind. Only by reflecting carefully on the sense of
pleasure in jhana and realizing that there was nothing to fear, that

there were no drawbacks in that type of pleasure, was he able to give himself wholeheartedly to the practice of jhana.

It's good to remember that whatever issues we have in the practice, the Buddha went through them all. It's not that there's something especially wrong with us. These are natural human tendencies. The Buddha was a human being and had to overcome natural human tendencies, too. So we're in good company. We've got his example to show that they *can* be overcome, and his assurance that we as human beings have what it takes to do it.

Finally there's the attitude of equanimity, which is useful in many ways. When we're working here in the meditation and the results aren't coming as fast as we'd like, equanimity teaches patience. It reminds us that the principle of action often requires that things take time. If you're working on something that takes time, try to develop equanimity. That makes it easier to be patient. Realize that things don't necessarily have to go the way you want them to right away. When you're willing to admit what the situation actually is, then you can actually act more effectively with it. Again, this is a matter of being patient, taking the time to understand what's going on.

So when we work at these sublime attitudes and bring them to the meditation, we find that they create a sense of patience, a sense of wellbeing, an ability to work at a task that takes time. Sometimes the practice seems to require that we do mindless things over and over again: Just bring the mind back to the breath, bring the mind back to the breath. Why? Don't ask questions right now, just bring the mind back to the breath. But be observant while you do it, because as you catch the mind going off, you can learn some very interesting things. You come to a point where you can see the mind beginning to move and you have the choice to go with it or not. Once you catch yourself at that point, then it's a lot easier to stay with the breath. You've learned an important lesson about how to read the movements of your mind.

The same principle applies to how you bring the mind back when you realize it's wandered off. Do you bring it back in a judgmental way or in a more judicious way? If you find that your attitude is judgmental, can you find other ways of simply bringing it back without all the extra baggage? Just very matter-of-factly bring it back and leave it at that. Just this simple process in and of itself teaches you a lot of lessons about the difference between being judgmental and being judicious. In other words, you try to understand, you try to look for patterns, so that the way you order the mind around or try to create some sense of control in here is actually effective.

The reason control freaks have a bad reputation is because they're ineffective. They're judgmental, they're not judicious in how they control things. Actually, control isn't a bad thing. But—as with being judicious—it has to be done skillfully. And that takes time, requires powers of observation. Watch what you're doing, watch the results. If things don't work, admit the fact and try something else. When you do this, you find it easier and easier to tell the difference between being judgmental and being judicious. At the same time, you start getting better results from your meditation, because you've taken the time to watch, to observe, to understand what's going on.

One of the main problems in modern life is that people have so little time. When they meditate, they want to cram as much of their meditation as possible into their little bits and pieces of spare time. Of course that aggravates the whole problem of being judgmental. So keep reminding yourself that meditation is a long-term project. When you have a sense of that long arc of time, it's a lot easier to sit back and work very carefully at the basic steps. It's like learning any skill. If, in one afternoon, you want to gain all the skills you're going to need to play tennis, you end up doing them all very sloppily and won't get the results you want. But if you realize that this may take time, you can work on one skill at a time: How do you keep your eye on the ball? How long is your backswing? Take the skill apart step by step by step and be willing to work on small things like this bit by bit by bit so that you really understand them deep down in your bones. That way, when the time comes to make choices, they'll be judicious choices, not judgmental choices, and you'll get the results you want.

Impossible Things

November, 2002

There's a character in *Through the Looking Glass* who says that he likes to think about two or three impossible things every morning before breakfast. It helps air out his mind. That's a good strategy for us as meditators—think about a couple of impossible things every day: that you're going to master concentration, you're going to taste the Deathless.

Of course these things, strictly speaking, are not impossible, but a lot of voices in our minds seem to insist that they are. So it's good to think about impossibilities every now and again to change the tone of the conversation.

Remind yourself that your life isn't already written in stone, that you're not a slave to fate or a little nameless cog in the big machine. You're actually a doer, a mover, a shaper. You can shape your life in the direction you want it to go.

The Buddha said that there are four types of action in the world: things we like to do that give good results, things we don't like to do that give bad results, things we like to do that give bad results, and things we don't like to do that give good results. The first two are no-brainers. Without even thinking, you do the things that you like to do and give good results. There's no conflict in the mind. The same holds true for things you don't like to do that give bad results. You don't want to do them. There's no discussion. The committee is unanimous.

The difficult actions are the ones you like to do but give bad results and the ones you don't like to do but give good results. The Buddha had an interesting comment on these two. He said they're a measure of a person's wisdom and discernment. He didn't say they're a measure of your willpower. You need to use discernment to do the things you don't like to do but give good results and to not do the things you like to do but give bad results. The discernment lies not only in seeing the connection between cause and effect in each case, but also in outmaneuvering the committee members who just want to do what they want to do regardless. It learns to see through the blockades that the mind puts up for itself, the difficulties it creates for itself, and figures out how to get past them.

One of the biggest difficulties we create for ourselves is our self-image. We notice that it's difficult to do things that are good for us and easy to do things that are not good for us, and we come to think that our nature is to be lazy, or that the lazy side of the mind is our true self, because the other side obviously takes effort. The lazy side of the mind is the one that just goes with the flow, so that must be who we truly are. That's what we think, but that kind of thinking is really self-destructive.

We may remember the times when we've done the right thing— when we've meditated, followed the precepts, lived in line with the Dhamma—but all we can think about is how much effort it took. So we say, "That must not truly be me. That must be somebody else. I must be the person who does things that are easy, I must be lazy, I must have very poor willpower." That kind of attitude is a huge misunderstanding. The things that are difficult are hard for everybody. Rather than creating a self-image about it, though, wise people just think, "How can I maneuver around this laziness? How can I maneuver around this negative attitude?" They experiment and try different approaches until they find what works.

This is what you have to try to do in your meditation. If you find yourself up against that kind of obstacle, learn to take your self-image apart. Realize that your self is not a given, the image itself is not a given. It's a pattern, it's a habit, this kind of self-imaging you have. If it gets in the way of what you really want, then no matter how much it screams that "this is your true self," you have to question it. You have to take it apart. Don't believe it.

No matter how much the mind may say it doesn't want to struggle, that's just one part of the mind. There's another part that does want to attempt the struggle, does want to have the strength, does want to see things through. The lazy side has sabotaged that by saying, "That's not really me." Well, who is this lazy side? Why would you want to identify with it? You have the choice.

Try to find the holes in its arguments, learn how to take things apart. You have to learn to deconstruct the negative habits in the mind. The first step is to question their truth, their validity. After all, the Buddha said that the mind can be trained, and that happiness comes from the training. If people couldn't change, there'd be no point in teaching the Dhamma. There'd be no point in trying to practice. The truth of the matter, though, is that we all have the potential for change. Each moment is a new moment, a moment with an element of freedom.

Then there's the part of the mind that says, "Okay, you can choose to do the right thing right now, but it's not going to last very long." You have to question that, too. The best way to question it is to choose to do the right thing for at least the next moment and the next moment and the next moment and then say, "See? I can do it." The negative side will come up with all kinds of other arguments, but you have to be determined not to listen to them, not to believe them. Try to figure out ways to undercut the part of the mind that does believe them.

It's kind of like internal politics. There are certain voices that come screaming at you all the time, and you've learned to give in to them, sometimes simply because of their force. If you stop and really look at them, though, you see that there's not much there that you'd really like to give in to. So you have to create other voices in the mind. The path is something you create, after all. It's something you put together. In technical terms it's *sankhata dhamma,* something you put together.

The question is not whether you naturally like it or not. That's one of the main, common misunderstandings in American Buddhism right now: this sense that you can choose whichever path you like and it won't matter because all the paths come out the same in the end. Well, there are paths that work, and there are paths that don't. A path you happen to like isn't necessarily going to take you where you really want to go.

So there has to be an element of struggle. There has to be an element of putting something new together, of not falling back into old ways. When you stop to think of it, when you fall into old ways there's an element of construction, you're creating that old sense of self over and over every time you give in to it. Is that the kind of self you want to create? You have the option to create something else.

For many of us, we don't like the responsibility because if we're responsible that means we're going to be responsible for our mistakes. So you have to ask, "Well, so what?" Everybody makes mistakes. Even the Buddha made mistakes before he became the Buddha. This is where we're all coming from.

This is why *sanghanussati,* recollection of the Sangha, is such a useful contemplation. Sometimes it's hard to compare yourself to the Buddha, but you can compare yourself to members of the noble Sangha. People who followed the Buddha's teachings were of all kinds. There were lepers, poor people, rich people, all kinds of people. One famous pair was Mahapandaka and Culapandaka. They were brothers. Mahapandaka was the older brother; Culapandaka, the younger brother. Mahapandaka was very smart, Culapandaka was very dumb, yet both of them became arahants. There are all kinds of people in the noble Sangha. Everyone in the noble Sangha has been where you are now, in terms of the strengths and weaknesses of their minds. What made the difference is that they finally decided that they were going to use those strengths to overcome those weaknesses. And the first step was simply thinking that it could be done. If they could do it, so can you. It may seem impossible, but you can get used to thinking impossible things.

After all, the Buddha was told that it was impossible, the idea that there could be a Deathless, that there could be something better than what he already had. There he was: wealthy, educated, good looking, powerful. He had all the sensual objects and pleasures that anyone could imagine, and he still wasn't satisfied. His family and friends said, "Don't kid yourself. The Deathless isn't possible. This is as good as it gets."

He said, "Well, if this is as good as it gets, then life is pretty miserable, because it's all going to fall apart someday." So he set out to find the impossible—and he found it. We may not feel up to comparing ourselves to the Buddha, but there are lots of noble disciples who must have felt at some point that true happiness must be an impossibility, that for them to change must be an impossible thing. But then one day they decided to do the impossible. That's how they ended up being members of the noble Sangha. The point being, of course, that what we think is impossible is not necessarily impossible. We've just allowed ourselves to be limited.

When I first ordained, I found that the scariest part of being ordained was that so much more was demanded of me. When you live in normal society, people's expectations, people's standards, are not all that high. It's not all that difficult to live up to them. But suddenly when there's the possibility of working for the Deathless, it seems overwhelming. There's part of the mind that wants to run back to the shelter of what seems easier to handle. But of course what's easier to handle also brings on more suffering.

As the Buddha said, "Lay life is hard. Life as a renunciate is hard." But at least life as a renunciate takes you someplace really worth going to. When you finally make up your mind that you're really going to train yourself, it makes that goal less of an impossibility.

So try to overcome that barrier in your mind that deep down someplace says, "I can't do this." Question it. Why would you want to believe that? Who in your mind is saying that? It's the part of the mind that doesn't want to make an effort. Do you want to identify with that part of the mind? You can if you want to, but you don't have to. You have the opportunity of identifying with better voices in the mind. It's your choice. No matter how impossible it may seem, it is your choice.

Contentment in the Practice

July, 2001

Every time you sit down to work with the breath, remember the story of the foolish, inexperienced cow. The cow is in a nice meadow on the hillside, has plenty of green grass and water, but sees another meadow over on another hillside and starts wondering, "What's the grass like over there? What's the water like over there?" And so because she's a foolish, inexperienced cow, she sets out. She doesn't know how to go down the hillside, cross over the ravine and go up the other hillside, so she gets lost in between. She doesn't get to the other hillside and can't get back to where she originally was.

This stands for the mind that, once it gets into a state of concentration, wonders where to go next to get something better. The trick is to learn how to stay in your meadow, so the grass has a chance to grow, so you have a chance to enjoy the water right where you already are. And the place where you are will develop into deeper and deeper states of concentration. This is why it's so important that before you start working with the breath here or there, adjusting it here or there, you find at least some spot where it's comfortable and focus on that.

To make another comparison, it's like starting a fire on a windy day. You have your tiny little flame, so you cup it in your hands and make sure that it doesn't get blown out. At the same time, you don't cut off the oxygen. You cup it in your hands just right, keeping that one little flame going, and after a while it will catch. Then it will spread throughout all the timber you've piled up. But it's important that you get that first little flame going.

The same with the breath: Find at least one little spot and stay right there for a while. It doesn't have to be a big spot, just a small spot. And content yourself with that small spot for the time being. Allow it to be comfortable. After a while it will catch. Then you can start spreading that sense of comfort throughout the body because you're working from a position of strength. You're working from a position of comfort, not a position of desperation or anxiety or restlessness, thinking that this has to be like that, or that has to be like this. Just content yourself with what you've got and allow it to grow. Content yourself at first with the small things, and ultimately, with practice, they'll grow into a greater and greater sense of wellbeing.

Remember that the word *jhana* comes from the verb *jhayati,* or *burning.* This verb isn't used to describe just any kind of burning; it's used to describe the burning of an oil lamp. When an oil lamp burns, the flame is steady. It may not be a big flame, but its steadiness is what helps it illuminate the room. You can read by it. If it were a flickering flame, you couldn't read by it, no matter how bright it was, for the shadows would be jumping all over the place. But the steadiness of the oil-lamp flame is what enables you to read even in an otherwise dark room.

It's the same with the state of your concentration. You stay steadily with one spot. The steadiness, the consistency of your gaze is what allows this one spot to become really comfortable. In the beginning it may not be all that comfortable, just an okay spot someplace in the body. The breath feels okay coming in, feels okay coming out. No big deal, nothing special. But you find, if you allow yourself to settle into it, that it can resolve a basic problem in the mind: the underlying tension where it's ready to jump at a moment's notice, like a cat settled in one spot but coiled up ready to spring. If you could take a picture of the mind in its everyday, normal state, that's what it would look like: a cat coiled ready to spring. When it lands on an object, part of it is ready to spring away from that object as soon as it doesn't like the object, as soon as the object turns into something unpleasant, because that's the way it's been dealing with objects all along.

But here you allow it to settle into one little spot and let that sense of tension in the mind melt away. You melt into the object of your concentration and then let that melting sensation spread into the body, all the way down to your fingers and toes. This way the meditation goes a lot better than if you're constantly fighting and figuring things out too much. You've got to learn how to apply just the right amount of pressure, just the right amount of pushing, not too much, not too little. The more sensitive you are in your meditation, the better it goes.

So you've got a meadow someplace in your body. It may not be a big one, but it's there. You don't sit around worrying about where the next meadow's going to be or what other meadows you have around you. Just stay right where you are and the grass will grow. The water will flow. And you find that the place where you are starts to develop. That's the kind of concentration you can really live with.

In other words, it's the kind of concentration you can pick up and take with you wherever you go, not where you prefashion things too much and preconceive things too much and have to do this and have to do that and adjust this and adjust that and it all becomes very theoretical. Just an inner sense of allowing it to feel just right, right here, to feel good right here, and wherever you go, you're still with "right here." You can identify where that good feeling is and carry it with you wherever you go. That's the kind of concentration that grows. It's the kind of concentration that seeps into your life and begins to make a difference in how you think, how you act, and how you speak, because it's there all the time. It doesn't require too much fashioning. It may require a little bit of looking after, but not based on what you've read in books. It's just a sense of wellbeing right here. You've got your little spot and you take it with you.

Ajaan Fuang once said that mindfulness and concentration are little tiny things but you've got to keep at them all the time. The statement sounded better in Thai because it was a pun. There's the word *nit*, which means little, but there's also the word *nit*—spelled differently but pronounced the same way—which means constantly. So concentration is a little tiny thing that you do constantly. When it comes from this beginning sense of wellbeing, it's a lot more stable. You can maintain it a lot longer. The sense of wellbeing begins to glow throughout the body and the mind when you allow it to happen, when you allow the grass to grow and the water to flow. Or, in terms of the image of the flame, when you give it enough space and protection to allow it to catch hold.

In one of Ajaan Lee's talks he says that big things have to start from little things. Sometimes you have to content yourself with just a little bit of concentration, a little comfortable spot, but you stick with it constantly. You plant one banana tree, and after a while it will grow and provide you with the seeds to plant more banana trees. So you take the seeds out of the banana—in Thailand they have bananas with seeds—you plant them, and after a while you've got a whole banana orchard. Or even better, mangoes: You've got one tree that you take really good care of. You don't yet worry about planting the rest of your land. You've got your one tree and after a while it gives mangoes, and bit by bit you can plant a whole orchard with the seeds you got from the fruit of the one tree. At the same time, you get to eat the flesh of the mangoes. You can enjoy yourself. After all, this is a part of the path, the part where the Buddha explicitly mentions rapture, pleasure, and ease as factors of the path. If you don't have that sense of wellbeing, the practice gets very dry.

As you're planting the mangoes and eating their flesh, you find that the path becomes a really nice place to be, a good path to follow—not only because you know it's going to take you to a good place, but also because it's a good path to be on while you're there. You're not going through the desert. You're going through orchards and lush countryside. If you learn to recognize which plants are food and which ones are medicine for which disease, there's plenty to keep you healthy and energized all along the way.

Patience

November, 2002

We're an impatient society. Everything has to be done *fast*, the results have to come *fast*, or else we lose interest quickly. It's because we're so impatient that we don't understand what patience is all about. When we're told to be patient, many times we think it's a sign that we shouldn't care about the results, that we don't have to be so committed to the practice, that we can let things take their course whenever they want to. We think that patience means a lack of resolution, a lack of dedication, that you're a carefree and indifferent about when things are going to come together, when the results are going to show.

That's not what patience means. Patience means sticking with the *causes* of your practice, no matter how long it takes to get the results. In other words, you're resolute in doing the practice, you stick with it, you stay with it, slow and steady.

Khanti, the Pali word we often translate as patience, also means *endurance.* It means that you stick with things even when they take a long time to show results. You don't get frustrated. You remind yourself: This a path that takes time. After all, we're unlearning a lot of habits that we've been indulging for who knows how long. So it only stands to reason that it's going to take time to unlearn those habits. The only way to unlearn them is to actually stick with the practice, to be resolute in what you're doing. This firm resolution is what's going to make the difference.

Ajaan Thate talks about being patient like farmers. Those of you who've never lived on a farm, even you know that farmers don't have an easy life. They work hard, especially in Thailand, where they don't have a lot of labor-saving devices. When the time comes to do what needs to be done, they have to do it quickly. In other words, when the rice grains are ready, you have to harvest them quickly before the mice get to them. You have to take care of them quickly, winnow the rice quickly before any late season rain comes to spoil it. So it's not a matter of being slow or casual, this patience of a farmer. The patience of a farmer is the sort that knows you can't plant the rice today and expect to have the grains ripened tomorrow. It's going to take time, and during that time it's going to require work.

Fortunately for farmers, they have experience. They know from previous years how long it takes. We, however, don't have that kind of experience. We're working on something new, developing new habits in the mind. Sometimes we read the passages in the *Satipatthana Sutta* about how you can gain Awakening in seven days if you're really dedicated, and we come away with unrealistic ideas about how quickly we should see results in order to deem our practice successful. This is not to say that it's not possible, but just that most of the people who could get results in seven days have already gotten results and gone to nibbana. That leaves the rest of us here muddling along—which doesn't mean we should be any less dedicated in our practice. We should just realize that it's going to take time.

Good things always take time. The trees with the most solid heartwood are the ones that take the longest to grow. So we do the practice, focusing on what we're doing, rather than getting into an internal dialogue about when the results are going to come, what they're going to be like, and how we can speed up the practice. Many times our efforts to speed things up actually get in the way. Our practice is pretty simple. Stay with the breath, allow the mind to settle in with the breath, be friends with the breath. Allow the breath to open up and get more and more gentle, more and more porous, so your awareness can seep into the breath. That's all you have to do.

Of course, we want to add things on top of that to make the results come faster, but the things we add on top get in the way. So try to keep things simple. Just stay with the breath. If the mind is going to get into any dialogue, engage in a dialogue about how the breath feels right now, reminding yourself to stay with breath, catching the mind when it's going to slip off. There's a lot of work to do, even when you try to keep it simple, just keeping the mind with the breath. As for whether the results are coming as quickly as you'd like or, when they come, whether they're going to stay as long as you'd like: That's going to depend on what you're doing right here with the breath. Our desire to have the results come, our desire to have them stay, is not going to keep them here. The actual doing of the practice is what will make the difference.

There's a passage in the texts where the Buddha talks about a hen incubating her eggs. Whether or not the hen has a desire for the eggs to hatch, they're going to develop. Whether or not she has a little dialogue about how quickly she wants them to come, and why aren't they coming any faster than this, all those little questions that she probably doesn't have the brain to ask.... Our problem is that we do have brains that ask those questions and they get in the way. If you're going to ask questions, ask questions about what you're doing right now. "Is that you wandering off? Where are you going? Are you looking for trouble? Or are you staying right here?" That's all you have to ask. Just be really consistent and resolute in sticking with what you know you have to do.

If you find yourself flagging, learn how to give yourself pep talks, encouraging yourself along the way. Do what you can to keep the mind right here as consistently and steadily as possible. Consistency is what builds up momentum. Although we'd like momentum to build up fast, sometimes our minds are pretty massive, and the massive minds are the ones that take time to accelerate. So try to streamline things as much as you can. Stay focused. Stay resolute in what you're doing.

As for the results, that's what you're patient about. Don't allow yourself to be patient or tolerant about vagrant thoughts that will pull you away from the breath. Patience relates to the process of causality in the sense that you can't push the results to appear unless the causes are right. Sometimes the causes take a while to come together. But you can rest assured that when they do they'll bring the results, without your having to concoct a lot of preconceived notions about them.

When they do come, don't abandon the causes. When the mind finally does get a sense that it's settling in, feeling comfortable, don't leave the breath to focus on the comfort. The comfort's there, you can think of it spreading through the body, but spread it through the body by means of the breath. If you abandon the breath, it's like letting the foundation of a house rot away. You like the house, it's a comfortable place, but if you don't look after the foundation you'll soon have no place to stay.

So the focus should always be on the causes, and you should apply yourself to the causes with as much commitment and resolution as you can muster. Let go of your thoughts about how long you've been practicing, what the results used to be in the past. Focus on what you're doing, totally on what you're doing, *right now.*

Training the Whole Mind

June, 2001

When we train the mind, it's not just a question of using a meditation technique to bludgeon the mind into the present moment. If that's our approach, the mind is going to start rebelling, finding ways of slipping around our defenses, because there are times when the meditation technique is right for the situation and times when it isn't. The times when it isn't: That's when the mind is going to rebel if you single-mindedly use just that one technique and don't have other techniques or approaches up your sleeve as well.

Meditation is not just a question of technique. In training the mind, you have to remember there's a whole committee in there. In the past the committee has had its balance of power, its likes and dislikes, and the politics among the various voices in your mind. Each of them has different tricks for pushing its agenda on the rest. So just as these defilements have lots of tricks up their sleeves, you as a meditator need to have lots of tricks up your sleeve, too.

One really basic trick is for when the mind says, "I've got to do this. I want to do that. I don't want to meditate." You've got to ask, "Well why?" And play kind of dumb, so that the mind really has to explain itself. It's like lesson number one in any journalism class: If you really want to get a good interview out of people, you have to play dumb, ask stupid questions, so that they think they have to explain things to you very carefully. And oftentimes they reveal all kinds of things they wouldn't have otherwise.

It's the same with your own mind. When greed, anger, and delusion come into the mind, they usually barge in with a lot of force and expect to push you right over. So one thing you have to do is to ask, "Well, why? Why should we follow that? Why should we want instant gratification?" And there will be an "of course-ness" to their answer the first time around. "Of course you want it this way. Of course you want it that way." "Well why?" If you're persistent in being block-headed like this, all the defilements will start revealing themselves. You'll see how shabby they are. You'll be able to get around them more easily.

It's like training a little child. Sometimes you have to be strict with the child, other times you have to offer rewards, patiently explain things. Other times you have to make up little games. In other words, you have to use your full psychology with the mind. But this time around you're not using it for the purpose of deception, which is what the mind ordinarily does with itself. You're using it for the purpose of truth and honesty, for what's really in your own best interest.

What does the wandering mind do for you? It gives a little bit of instant gratification and then that gratification goes, with nothing left to show for itself. If you keep allowing this to happen, where are you going to pick up the skills you'll really need when aging, illness, and death hit with full force? This is why the Buddha stressed the principle of heedfulness all the time. We can't just spend our time sniffing the flowers and looking at the sky. There's work to be done. When the mind is untrained, it causes us a lot of unhappiness. If the mind is well trained, if it's more tractable, it can bring a lot of happiness our way.

In order for that to happen, you have to learn how to psyche yourself into the mood to meditate. Once it starts meditating and begins to see the results, it gets more willing and tractable—most of the time. Then there are times it starts rebelling all over again, totally irrationally. So you've got to sit down with it again, work things through with it again, to see exactly what issue got covered up the last time around and is only now getting exposed.

This is one of the ways in which you learn a lot about your defilements. It's not that you have to wait for a totally solid concentration before you can see the defilements clearly. A lot of learning about the defilements lies in learning how to struggle with them as you bring the mind to stillness. You begin to see: "Oh, this is how greed works, this is how aversion works, this is how I've fallen for this stuff before in the past. Well, this time around I'm not going to fall."

Sometimes it's like a battle. Other times it's more a question of learning how to work together in a way that's for your own best interests: how to be a mediator, a negotiator, or a patient teacher. You've got to have lots of ways of relating to the different elements in your mind. The times when you can win the defilements over to your side: That's when it's best. Your desire turns into a desire to practice. Your hatred turns into a hatred of the defilements. You learn how to use the energy of these things for your own true benefit.

That's when you can be said to be a discerning mediator. You can't gain insight simply by following the rules. Somebody says, "For insight you need to do one, two, three, four, five, six, and seven. So you do one, two, three, four, five, six, seven without any thinking, without any reflection on what you're doing, and yet that doesn't give you any true insights. It gives you pre-programmed insights sometimes, but the actual startling new understandings that can come through the meditation don't happen because you're too busy following the directions.

The directions are there for you to apply to the mind and then to observe, to look at what happens, to reflect on what happens, to make adjustments. Make the meditation your own and not just somebody else's bulldozer running through your head. After all, the big issue is how you relate to yourself, how you relate to the body, how you relate to feelings, perceptions, thought-fabrications, and consciousness. That's the area where you're causing yourself suffering, so that's the area where you've got to gain sensitivity and insight. Nobody else can get into your head and straighten these things out for you. You use the techniques of meditation to see what they reveal about the mind. Then you build on those lessons so that the meditation becomes your own.

In Thai, they have a word for practice—*patibat*—which also means looking after someone, to attend to someone's needs. In the practice of the Dhamma you're looking after your own mind, attending to your own mind's needs. It's not so much that you're learning about Buddhism. You're learning about your own mind, looking after your own mind. That's when the meditation really starts showing its value. It rearranges all the power balances in the mind so that truth begins to take over, wisdom begins to take over, discernment begins to take charge. These become the big powers in your mind, the ones in charge of any discussion.

When that's the kind of mind you have, it's a really good mind to live in. We live in physical places only for a certain amount of time but in our own minds all the time. Try to make the mind a good place to live so that, no matter what else happens outside, at least the mind is on proper terms with itself, not fighting itself, not doing stupid things that aren't in its own best interest. Get so that it really does know how to deal with the aggregates as they arise, how to deal with pain so it doesn't turn it into suffering, how to deal with pleasure so it doesn't turn it into suffering. Get so that the mind develops a basic intelligence in sorting itself out, managing itself, so that all your mental powers suddenly become powers you can truly put to good use.

As we were saying today, there are times when, for your own good, you don't want to be focused on the breath. There are things you have to think about, things you've got to plan for, things you have to ponder, where you take all the powers of the mind you've trained in concentration and put them to other uses. That way the benefits of the concentration permeate your whole life, everything you do.

So it's an all-around training, not just learning to relate to the breath, but learning how to relate to everything else going on in the mind as well, so that skillful thoughts take over and unskillful thoughts get left behind. That's when you can say that the meditation is a whole-mind process. That's when it gives results penetrating throughout your whole life. The committee members learn how to live together. The unskillful ones get outvoted. The ones who should be in charge, the skillful qualities, take over and run the show in such a way that nobody suffers.

The Grain of the Wood

November 9, 1996

The Buddha teaches that there are two sides to the path of practice: the side of developing and the side of letting go. And it's important that you see the practice in both perspectives, that your practice contains both sides. If you practice just letting go, you'll throw away the baby with the bath water. Everything good will get thrown out because you let go of everything and leave nothing left. On the other hand, if yours is just a practice of developing and working and doing, you miss the things that happen on their own, that happen when you do let go.

So an important part of the practice is realizing which is which. This is what discernment is all about, realizing which qualities in the mind are skillful, the ones that are your friends, and which qualities are unskillful, the ones that are your enemies. The ones that are your friends are those that help make your knowledge clearer, make you see things more clearly—things like mindfulness, concentration, and discernment, together with the qualities they depend on: virtue, morality, persistence. These are the good guys in the mind. These are the ones you have to nurture, the ones you have to work at. If you don't work at them, they won't come on their own.

Some people think that practice is simply a matter of letting the mind go with its own flow, but the flow of the mind tends to flow down, just as water flows downhill, which is why the mind needs to be trained. In training the mind, we're not creating the unconditioned or unfabricated in the mind. It's more like polishing wood. The grain is already there in the wood but, unless you polish it, it doesn't shimmer, it doesn't shine. If you want to see the beauty of the grain, you have to polish it, to work at it. You don't create the grain, but the polishing is what brings out the grain already there. If you don't polish it, it doesn't have the same shimmer, it doesn't have the same beauty as it does when it's polished.

So practicing the Buddha's path is like polishing away at the mind to see what's of real value there within the mind. That's what the mindfulness, the persistence, the ardency, and all the other terms the Buddha uses that suggest effort and exertion: That's what they're for. This is why we have rules in the practice: rules in terms of the precepts, rules for the monks to follow. They provide work for the mind, and it's good work. They're not just "make-work" rules. When you hold by the rules, when you hold by the precepts, the result is that you learn an awful lot about the mind at the same time you're making life a lot easier for yourself and the people around you. In the beginning it may seem harder to have the rules to follow, but once you start living by them, they open up all kinds of possibilities that weren't there before when everything was confined by the riverbanks of your old habits, going along with the flow.

This is why there has to be effort. This is why there has to be work in the practice. As the Buddha said, right effort has four sides. Abandoning is only one of the four. There's also preventing—preventing unskillful things from arising. When unskillful things have arisen, those are the things you abandon. Then there's the effort to give rise to skillful qualities, and the effort to maintain them once they are there. You develop these skillful qualities and then you keep them going so that they develop to higher and higher levels. So sometimes, when you're reflecting on your practice, it's useful to focus on exactly what you're developing here—the good qualities like mindfulness and alertness. At other times it's helpful to focus on the things you have to let go of, the things you have to work at preventing.

You see right effort very easily when doing concentration practice because you have to focus on where you want the mind to be, to be aware of where you don't want it to be, and also to be ready to fight off anything that's going to come in to disturb your stillness of mind. When you're focusing on your meditation topic, you pick it up and say that this is what you're going to focus on for the next hour. By doing this you're giving rise to skillful qualities. And then you try to keep your focus there. You've got to keep reminding yourself that this is what you're doing here. You're not just sitting; you're sitting here to develop the mind. So you keep your mind on the topic you've chosen, like the breath, and then you work at bringing the mind back whenever it slips off, bringing it here, keeping it here, at the same time being aware that any moment it can slip off again.

This second level of awareness is what keeps you from drifting off obliviously and then coming back to the surface five minutes later, suddenly realizing that you were off who-knows-where in the mean time. If you're prepared for the fact that the mind can leave at any point, then you can watch for it. In other words, you're watching both the breath and the mind, looking for the first sign that the mind is going to leap off onto something else. This is a heightened level of awareness that allows you to see the subtle stirrings in the mind.

The mind is often like an inchworm standing at the edge of a leaf. Even though the inchworm's back feet may still be on this leaf, its front feet are up in the air, swaying around, searching around for another leaf to land on. As soon as that other leaf comes, *boomph,* it's off. And so it is with the mind. If you're not aware of the fact that it's getting ready to leave the breath, it comes as a real surprise when you realize that you've slipped off someplace else. But when you have a sense of when the mind is beginning to get a little bit antsy and ready to move, you can do something about it.

In other words, you can't be complacent in the practice. Even if the mind seems to be staying with the breath, sometimes it's ready to move on, and you've got to have that second level of awareness going as well so that you can be aware both of the breath and of the mind together—so that you have a sense of when the mind is snug with its object and when it's beginning to get a little bit loose. If you see it loosening its grip, do what you can to make it more snug. Is the breath uncomfortable? Could it be more comfortable? Could it be finer? Could it be longer, shorter, whatever? Explore it.

The mind is telling you on its own that it isn't happy there anymore. It wants to move.

So look at the quality of the breath and then turn around and look at the quality of the mind—this sense of boredom, this wanting to move. What's actually causing it? Sometimes it comes from the breath, and sometimes it's just a trait that arises in the mind, a trait that stirs up trouble. Try to be sensitive to what's going on, to see whether the problem is coming from the mind or the object the mind is focused on. If it's coming from a simple sense of boredom that's moved in, let the boredom move on. You don't have to latch onto it. You don't have to identify with it, saying that it's *your* boredom. As soon as you identify with the boredom, the mind has left the breath and is on the boredom. Even though the breath may be there in the background, the boredom has come into the forefront. Your inchworm has moved off to the other leaf.

So if the mind is getting antsy and saying, "Well, move. Find something new," refuse for a while and see what happens. What is the strength lying behind that need to move? What's giving it power? Sometimes you'll find that it's actually a physical sensation someplace in the body that you've overlooked, so work on that. Other times it's more an attitude, the attitude that you picked up someplace that said, "Just sitting here not thinking about anything is the most stupid thing you can do. You aren't learning anything, you aren't picking up anything new. Your mind isn't being exercised." Ask yourself, "Where is that voice coming from?" It's coming from somebody who never meditated, who didn't understand all the good things that come from being still in the present moment.

Only when the mind is really still right here can it begin to resonate with the body. When there's a resonance between the breath and the mind, it gives rise to a much greater sense of wholeness and oneness. This is the positive aspect of the practice that you want to focus on, because if the mind is one place and the body someplace else, there's no resonance. It's as if they were singing two completely different tunes. But if you get them together, it's like having one chord with lots of overtones. And then you come to appreciate how, when there's this sense of resonance between the body and mind, you begin to open up. You begin to see things in the mind and in the body that you didn't see before. It's healing for both the body and the mind. It's also eye-opening in the sense that the more subtle things that were there suddenly appear. You gain a sense of appreciation for this, that this is a very important thing to do with the mind. The mind needs this for its own sanity, for its own health.

So when the mind starts getting antsy and wants to move around and think about things and analyze things, and it starts telling you that you're stupid to sit here and not think, remind it that not everything has to be thought through, not everything has to be analyzed. Some things have to be experienced directly. When you analyze things, where does the analysis come from? It comes mostly from your old ignorant ways of thinking. And what we're doing as we get the mind to settle down is to put those ways of thinking and those ways of dividing up reality aside. For a state of concentration you want to get the mind together with the body and to foster a sense of oneness, a sense of resonance between the two.

Once they've had chance to be together, *then* you can begin to see how things begin to separate out on their own. And this is a totally different way of separating. It's not the kind of separating that comes from ordinary thinking. It's actually seeing that even though the body and mind are resonating, they are two separate things, like two tuning forks. You strike one tuning fork and put another one next to it. The second tuning fork picks up the resonance from the first one, but they're two separate forks. Once the body and mind have had a chance to resonate for a while, you begin to see that they are two separate things. Knowing is different from the object of knowing. The body is the object; the mind is the knowing. And this way, when they separate out, they don't separate out because you have some preconceived notion of how they should be. You watch it actually happening. It's a natural occurrence. It's like the grain of the wood: When you polish it, the grain appears, but not because you designed the grain. It's been there in the wood all along.

The same with your meditation: You're simply giving yourself a chance really to see your experience of body and mind for what it is instead of coming in with preconceived notions about how things should get divided up, how things should be analyzed. There's a natural separation line between name and form, body and mind. They come together, but they're separate things. When you learn how to allow them to separate out, that's when real discernment comes in.

This is why the discernment that comes with concentration is a special kind of discernment. It's not your ordinary mode of thinking. It comes from giving things a chance to settle down. Like a chemical mixture: If everything gets jostled around, the two chemicals are always mixed together and you can't tell that there are two in there. There seems to be just the one mixture. But if you let the mixture sit for a while, the chemicals will separate. The lighter one will rise to the top; the heavier one will settle to the bottom. You'll see at a glance that there actually are two separate chemicals there. They separate themselves out on their own because you've created the conditions that allow them to act on their own.

The same with the mind: A lot of things begin to separate out on their own if you simply give the mind a chance to be still enough and you're watchful enough. If you're not watchful, the stillness drifts off into drowsiness. So you need the mindfulness together with the stillness for this to happen properly.

With the stillness, you're letting go of a lot of nervous activity, you're letting go of a lot of unskillful things in the mind. With the mindfulness, you're developing the skillful qualities you need to see clearly. This is how the letting-go and the knowing come together. When the Buddha discusses the four noble truths, he talks about the task appropriate to each. Your task with regard to craving, the second noble truth, is to let it go. Then there's a third noble truth, which is the cessation of suffering. And what is that? It's the letting-go of the craving. And your task with regard to that truth is to be aware of it, to realize it, as it's happening. So the task for this third truth is actually a double one: knowing together with the letting-go, and this makes all the difference in the world. Most of the time when we let go of craving we're not aware of what's happening, so it's nothing special. It's just the ordinary way of life as we move from one craving to another. But when the mind has been still enough, and the mindfulness well-developed enough, then when the craving gets abandoned you're aware of it as well, and this opens up something new in the mind.

This is why the factors of the noble eightfold path fall into two types: the ones that develop and the ones that let go. The ones that let go abandon all the mind's unskillful activities that obscure knowledge. The developing ones are the ones that enable you to see clearly: right view, right mindfulness, right concentration. They all work at awareness, so that you can know clearly what's actually happening in the present moment.

So there are these two sides to the practice, and you want to make sure that you're engaged in both sides for your practice to be complete. It's not just a practice of relaxing and letting go, and it's not just a practice of staying up all night and meditating ten hours at a stretch, really pushing, pushing, pushing yourself. You have to find a balance between clear knowing and effort, a balance between developing and letting go, knowing which is which and how to get that balance just right. That's the skill of the practice. And when you have both sides of the practice perfectly balanced, they come together and are no longer separate. You've got the mind in a perfectly clear state where the knowing and the letting-go become almost the same thing.

But the balance doesn't occur without practice. You may ask, "Why do we keep practicing? When do we get to perform?" Well, we're practicing for the time when ultimately we can master these things. When the practice gets balanced, the path performs, and that's when things really open up in the mind.

A Good Dose of Medicine

November 13, 1996

The Buddha often compared himself to a doctor, healing the diseases of the hearts and minds of his listeners. Now, we normally think about heart disease as meaning hardening of the arteries, and mental disease as insanity, but he said the real diseases of the heart, the real diseases of the mind, are three: passion, aversion, and delusion. They burn like a fever in the heart, a fever in the body. And the reason he taught about these diseases is because there *is* a way to gain release from them. If they were impossible to cure, he wouldn't have bothered to teach. So we have to learn to take his teaching as treatment for our own hearts, our own minds. That's when we're using them properly.

Treating these kinds of diseases is in some way similar to treating ordinary mental diseases, ordinary bodily diseases. And in some ways it's different.

With ordinary diseases, the doctor can give you medicine, you take the medicine, and that's it. With the Buddha's treatment, though, *you* are the one who administers the cure. You simply learn about the cure from the Buddha. As he says, he simply points out the way, but you're the one who actually has to carry through and administer the treatment to yourself. So you're both the doctor and the patient—you're a student doctor. You're learning the treatment. Sometimes the symptoms of the disease don't quite match what's printed in the texts, don't quite sound like the things you've heard people say: That's why you need an experienced doctor to help you along. But also you need your own ingenuity because there are times, as in a hospital, when the experienced doctor isn't on call. Sometimes a really drastic case comes in and there's nobody but interns around. The interns have to figure out what to do on their own. So it's not simply a matter of following what's in the books. You also have to learn how to apply the teachings to all kinds of unexpected situations, to learn which teachings are the basic principles and which are secondary details.

The similarity between the two types of diseases—outer diseases and inner diseases—is that in both cases there are two kinds of sources for the disease: inner and outer. Some bodily diseases you can blame on germs. They come in from the outside and they wreak a lot of havoc in the body. But on a more basic level the question is, "Why do the germs take over?"— because sometimes you have enough resistance to fight them off and sometimes you don't. In this sense the basic cause comes from inside, from your inner lack of resistance.

The same holds true with the mind. Many times we blame problems within the mind on things from outside—what other people do, what other people say, the general atmosphere around us, the values we grew up with, the things we learned as children. And these do play a role, but the most important problem is what comes from the mind. Why is it susceptible to those influences? After all, you find some people staying in a certain environment and they're perfectly okay, they pick up no negative influences, while other people get into the same environment and come out all warped. Two kids growing up in the same family hear the same lessons from their parents but take away totally different messages. This is because of what you bring to life when you come, what weak points and what strong points are already there in the mind.

So you have to focus in on the mind as the main problem. You can't go blaming things outside. If the mind had really good powers of resistance, a really good immune system, nothing could stir it to passion, nothing could stir it to anger, nothing could stir it to delusion. Fortunately, you can train the mind develop that immunity. That's the kind of mind you want to develop. That's the mind that the Buddha defines as health. This is why the training focuses inside, looking at your own mind and seeing where things set it off.

When germs come into the mind, where is your resistance strong and where is it weak? What is your line of resistance? This is what we're developing in the meditation: lines of resistance. Concentration, virtue, generosity: these are all our first lines of resistance against the invading germs.

Sitting here with our eyes closed, instead of trying to change things outside, we change things inside. Some people think that the practice is simply a matter of learning how to accept everything just as it is. Well, some things you do accept and some you don't. You learn to accept the fact that the outside world is going to be the way it is. There are always going to be external problems. And the phrase "outside world" here doesn't refer just to other people. Your own body is part of the outside world from the point of view of the Dhamma. And the body contains aging, illness, and death. That's the nature of the body. You can't change that, but what you *can* change is the mind. This is where you can't just sit around and be equanimous, accepting the mind as it is. You've got to accept that the mind has the potential to change. So you've really got to stir yourself to look into the mind, to see which potentials need to be weakened and which ones need to be enhanced.

This is where right effort comes in—when you learn how to distinguish skillful and unskillful states in the mind. The skillful ones are the ones that can keep up your resistance against greed, anger, and delusion. The unskillful ones are the ones that give in, the ones that are susceptible to infection. And because delusion is part of the problem, the first thing you need to learn is how to distinguish which states are skillful and which ones aren't. This is why you need instructions. This is why you need a technique in your meditation—you've got a focal point, the breath, as a measuring stick for the movements of the mind. You watch the breath as it's coming in and going out, and you notice when you get pulled away from it: That's a good measure of when the mind is being influenced by something. If you don't have this kind of focus, it's hard to tell when anger comes and when it goes. There's nothing to measure it against. Like the clouds in the sky: You can't tell how fast they're moving unless you've got something still and solid on the ground to use as your reference point—a tree, a telephone pole. If you focus on that one point, then you can see whether the clouds are moving north or south, and how fast they're going in relation to that point.

It's the same with the mind once it has a focal point like the breath: As soon as your attention gets pulled away from the breath, you know something has happened. Then you check to see what it is. In the beginning you simply notice what it is and—realizing that if you follow that, you're drifting away from where you want to be—you bring the mind back. This is on the basic level of just getting the mind to learn how to be still for a while, how to stick with your original intention to stay centered, and how to settle down. But as your powers of concentration, your powers of mindfulness get stronger and stronger, you find you can actually investigate what's pulling you away—or what *would* have pulled you away if you hadn't caught yourself in time. This is when your powers of resistance are getting stronger: when you begin to see exactly how you got hooked to that pull.

It's as if your mind is covered with Velcro hooks and you investigate to see what comes along and ends up stuck in them. Actually, those little Velcro hooks are choices. They're not necessary. You don't have to get stuck on things. There is actually a place in the mind where you're making a *choice* to latch on. Only when things get really still in the mind and your awareness is really clear can you see that choice as an act—that you made the choice to lower your resistance and latch onto the germs when you didn't have to. That's where you can let go. One, you see the drawbacks of the diseases caused by the germs and, two, you realize that you don't really have to come down with them. They're not really necessary. When you can identify the particular disease patterns, they will never be necessary. They seem necessary only when you can't conceive of anything else. "Things have to be that way," or so the mind tells itself. If the mind had to be that way, there would be no purpose in meditating, there would be no purpose in the Buddha's teaching. He could have sat around under the Bodhi tree for the rest of his life and just enjoyed the bliss of Awakening. He realized, though, that teaching would serve a purpose. So that's what we're doing—we're carrying out that purpose, putting his teachings into practice so we can gain the results that he wanted to see from the effort he put into his teaching.

All this comes under right effort, realizing when you have skillful states, realizing when you have unskillful states, and being determined that once an unskillful state has arisen you're not going to feed it, you're not going to follow along with it. Some people have problems with this, especially with the issue of struggling or effort or having a goal. The problem, though, doesn't lie with effort or goals in and of themselves. It lies with your attitude toward them. You need to have a healthy attitude toward this struggle. You need to have a healthy attitude toward the effort, toward the goal, because the goal is what gives you a direction in life. Without goals, life would just be floundering around, like fish flopping around in a puddle.

So you need to have a direction. You realize that maybe this is a bigger task than other tasks you have taken on, so you don't berate yourself for not getting to the goal immediately or not catching on right away. You learn through experience what your pace is and you stick to it. Sometimes you push yourself a little too hard in order to *know* what it means to push yourself too hard, and then you let off. And you find that you tend to vacillate back and forth between pushing too hard and not pushing enough, but as long as you're sensitive to this fact you begin to get a better and better sense of what "just right" is.

When the Buddha talks about the Middle Way, it's not necessarily what our preconceived notions of the Middle Way are. You have to test them. And the effort required is not blind effort. Right effort involves using your eyes: knowing what's skillful in the mind, what's unskillful, being determined to let go of anything unskillful that arises in the mind, and trying to prevent more unskillful things from arising in the mind. At the same time, you try to realize when skillful qualities have appeared. You try to maintain them, develop them, make them strong.

So there's both the letting-go and the developing, and the function of discernment is to tell when which is appropriate. You have to listen very carefully to what's happening in the mind, watch things in the mind, be observant. This is why a lot of the meditation instructions throw things back on you, on your own powers of observation, because only by developing those powers can you develop the discernment you're going to need.

Sometimes in the Buddha's teachings, it's almost as if he purposely leaves a few blanks, doesn't explain everything, leaves things for you to figure out on your own, because if everything were handed to you on a platter where would your discernment get engaged? How would it develop? You'd be a restaurant critic, picky and choosy about what's served to you, but totally ignorant about how to fix the food yourself. So sometimes the Buddha gives the teachings as riddles, and your willingness to try to figure them out, make mistakes, come back and try again, is what will make you grow. This is the healthy attitude toward right effort, realizing that sometimes it's going to take a lot of persistence, a lot of endurance, a lot of tenacity.

But not always. There are times when it gets very easy and enjoyable, and everything seems to flow. So you learn to adjust your effort so that it's just right for whatever the situation. That's when right effort is really right, when you start getting your own sense of how things vary and how things need to be adjusted. That's when the practice becomes more and more your own practice, the practice you've made your own, not just something that somebody outside is telling you to do. And this is where you turn from a student doctor into an experienced doctor.

Luckily with the diseases of the mind, it's not the case that your patients are all going to die. This particular patient, the mind, keeps coming back. So there's room for mistakes—but you can't be too complacent. After all, you're the patient. You're the one who suffers from the mistakes. Some of those mistakes can lead you down a path that ends up far away, and it'll be a long time before you find your way back. So again you need an attitude of balance: You don't berate yourself for not attaining the goal, but at the same time you don't get complacent.

Much of the practice is this one issue: figuring out where that balance is. Other people can help give you pointers, but you yourself really have to listen to your own practice, look carefully at the results as they come—because this ability to see cause and effect in the mind is what lies at the essence of discernment, and discernment is what makes all the difference. It's the ultimate medicine in the Buddha's medicine box—yet he can't just hand it to you. It's like an herbal medicine that you have to grow yourself. He describes it and tells you how to find it, how to grow it, and then how to take it.

So get used to this image that you're both the doctor and the patient, and learn to have a very strong sense of the doctor looking after the patient. Don't identify totally with the patient because if you do it's hard to see a cure, hard to see even the possibility of a cure. But if you have the attitude of the doctor, there has to be a notion of what health is and how to recognize illness whenever it shows its face. At the same time, you have to develop the ability to step back and look at the whole situation to figure out the cure.

Here's another image: Ann Landers. People who write letters to Ann Landers are so thoroughly immersed in their problems that they can't step back. They have trouble even formulating a letter. But all Ann Landers has to do is read the letter once it's formulated and usually she can give an answer right off the bat because she's not immersed in the situation. From her perspective, the issue is already formulated. Her job is not all that hard. You'll find your own practice gets a lot easier too when you can step back to recognize the problem and articulate it to yourself. Once the problem is clearly delineated, you've got your answer. As in the case of the doctor, the real difficulty lies in learning to diagnose the illness. Once you've got the diagnosis right, the choice of medicine is easy.

So the first step is learning how to be the doctor. Identify at least part of your mind as the doctor. This is the part you want to train. And the funny thing is that in training the doctor, the patient gets cured.

Life in the Buddha's Hospital

March, 2002

The Dhamma is like medicine. You can see this from the way the Buddha teaches. He starts off with the four noble truths, which are very much like an analysis of how to care for a disease. In his case, he's offering a cure for the basic disease of the mind: the suffering that comes from craving and ignorance. That's what we've got to cure. So he analyzes the symptoms of the disease, diagnoses it, explains its causation, discusses what it's like to be free of the disease, and then shows a path of treatment that leads to the end of the disease, to a state of health.

It's important that we keep this in mind as we practice here together: We're working on the diseases of our own minds. Each of us has illnesses. And although the basic causes of illness are the same—craving, ignorance—our cravings are different. Our particular brands of ignorance are different as well. This is why we have to make allowances for each other, because different people have to undergo different courses of treatment.

It's like going into a hospital. It's not the case that everyone in the hospital has the same diseases. Some people have cancer, some have heart diseases, some have liver diseases. Some people have diseases from eating too much, some from eating too little. There are all kinds of different diseases in the hospital. And it's the same way here in the monastery. We each have our own particular diseases. And our duty here is to take care of our own diseases without picking up diseases from other people—and at the same time not getting upset that somebody else is taking a different kind of medicine than you are. Each of us has his or her own diseases requiring specific kinds of medicine. Some medicines are bitter and unpleasant to take; other medicines are a lot easier to swallow. So each of us has his or her own course of treatment. It's important that we pay attention to our own course of treatment, and not worry about the treatments of others.

If some people don't seem to be recovering from their diseases as fast as you would like them to, well, again, it's *their* disease. Try to keep this is mind. Remember what Ajaan Lee says: *"When you look inside, it's Dhamma. When you look outside, it's the world."* And it's not just that you're a detached observer looking at the world. Your whole mind becomes the world as well when you start focusing outside. "This person does that, this person does this": That's the world, even if you use the categories of the Dhamma to judge the person. You've taken the Dhamma and you've turned it into the world. So you've got to keep your gaze focused inside.

In other words, when you get upset at someone else, what is this quality of being upset? Focus on that. The events in the mind are the important issues. Those are the things causing your own illness. Do you want to cure your own illness or to aggravate it? Keep this question in mind as you practice.

As we live together and practice together, we see each other a lot, but try to make that fact have the least possible impact on the mind. Try to turn your gaze inside. Even when you're looking outside, you want your focus to be inside: "How is your mind reacting to this? How is your mind reacting to that?" This is part of restraint of the senses. Several years back we had an elderly visitor from Thailand who was very serious about practicing restraint of the senses. She kept her eyes down and hardly talked to anyone. And then she overheard other people talking about how stuck up and unfriendly she was because she was trying to be so quiet and unresponsive. So she came to me to complain about how other people were not respecting her restraint of the senses. Of course, what kind of restraint is that, getting upset over what other people are saying about you?

Restraint is purely an internal matter. As you go through life you have to hear things, see things, taste things, touch things, think about things. The point of restraint is that you don't make those things the main focus. The process of how the mind reacts to the seeing, how it directs the seeing, and so on with the other senses: *that* should be your focus. If issues come up and aggravate the illness in the mind, how are you going to deal with it? The Buddha laid out a lot of medicines for us to choose. The chant on the 32 parts of the body: That's basically a reminder of his medicines for dealing with attachment to your own body and lust for the bodies of others. The chant on the four sublime attitudes: That's for dealing with not only anger but also with resentment, jealousy, any cruel intentions in your mind. Many times you can get worked up about things totally beyond your control: That's when you should reflect on the principle of kamma to develop equanimity.

There are antidotes for all these diseases, and our duty here is to use them. Because, after all, who's suffering because of our diseases? Other people may be suffering to some extent, but *we're really suffering*. We suffer very little from what other people do, and a great deal from the lack of skill in our own minds.

In the Canon the Buddha talks about how people should not give in to craving and conceit, and when we look at other people it's obvious that he's right. Their craving and conceit are obviously causing trouble. The trick, though, lies in seeing our *own* craving, our *own* conceit. If you find yourself using these teachings to judge other people, stop and ask yourself: "Well, wait a second. Am I the National Bureau of Standards?"

Then turn around and look at yourself. What about your own craving? You want things to be a certain way and then they aren't the way you want them to be. This is a very important lesson I learned with Ajaan Fuang. He always seemed to fall sick at times that were extremely inconvenient for me. I'd have some project going on around the monastery, and it always seemed that just when I was really getting into the project, he got sick and I had to drop everything to look after him. I began to notice the sense of frustration growing within me and I finally realized, "Hey, wait a minute. If I let go of the desire to finish that project, things go a lot more easily." At the same time, if I let go of my desire for him to care for his illness in the way I thought best, it made things a lot easier around the monastery. Especially for me, and—probably in no small measure—for him as well.

When you start running into that reality, realize: Your cravings are the things that are making you suffer, so those are the things you have to let go of. When you let go, you find you can live with all kinds of situations. Not that you become lazy or apathetic, just letting things be whatever way they want to be. You become selective: Where can you make a difference? Where can you not make a difference? Where is your craving helping you in the path? Where is it getting in the way? You have to learn how to be selective, how to be skillful in where you direct your wants, where you direct your aspirations. Again, the problem is not outside. The problem is inside. We do suffer to some extent from things outside, but the reason we suffer is because things inside are unskillful. That's what we have to work on. Once the inside problem is dealt with, the outside problems don't touch us at all.

Conceit is another troublemaker. Conceit is not just puffing yourself up and thinking you're better than other people. According to the Buddha, it's the tendency of the mind to compare itself with others. Even if you say, "I'm worse than that other person," or, "I'm equal to that other person," that's conceit. There's an "I" there: the "I-making, mine-making, and tendency to conceit." That's a lot of the problem right there, a major cause of disease.

The Buddha describes the sense of "I am" as the underlying cause for the mind's tendency to proliferate ideas, its tendency to make differentiations, to complicate things, and all the categories and conflicts that come from those complications: These all start with the "I am." The basic verbalization of craving also starts with "I am." It then goes on to "I was," "I will be," or "Am I? Am I not?" and all the other questions that come up from putting the "I" and the "am" together and then identifying with them. You start comparing this "I am" to other people's, to your sense of what they are. So either you're better than they are, or you're equal, or you're worse. Whichever side you come down on, though, it's just a big troublemaker all around.

Just keep remembering: Other people's diseases are *their* diseases. They've got to cure them. They've got to take their medicine. Your diseases are yours—your prime responsibility. And if the person next to you in the hospital room is not taking his medicine properly, that's his problem. You can be helpful and encourage him, but there comes a time when you have to say, "Okay, that's his issue. I've got my own disease to take care of." This way it's a lot easier for all of us.

When these attachments, cravings, and conceits don't get in the way, then any place you practice becomes an ideal place to practice. People often ask, "Where is the best place to practice?" And the answer is, "Right here in the here-and-now." It's actually the only place you can practice. But you can do things to make the here-and-now a better place to practice wherever you are, both for yourself and for the people around you. It's dependent not so much on changing things outside as it is on changing your inner attitudes. That way the place where we're practicing becomes a good place to practice for us all.

Vows

October, 2002

When you read Ajaan Lee's autobiography, you notice the number of times he made vows: vowing to sit all night, vowing to meditate so many hours, vowing to do this, vowing to do without that. The word for vow in Thai is *"adhithaan,"* which is also translated as determination. You make up your mind, you're determined to do something. Making determinations like this gives strength to your practice. Otherwise you just sit and meditate for a while and when the going gets tough—"Well, that's enough for today." You don't push your limits. As a result you don't get a taste of what lies outside the limits of your expectations.

As the Buddha said, the purpose of the practice is to see what you've never seen before, realize what you've never realized before, and many of these things you've never seen or realized lie outside the limits of your imagination. In order to see them, you have to learn how to push yourself more than you might imagine. But this has to be done with skill. That's why the Buddha said that a good determination involves four qualities: discernment, truth, relinquishment, and peace.

Discernment here means two things. To begin with, it means setting wise goals: learning how to recognize a useful vow, one that aims at something really worthwhile, one in which you're pushing yourself not too little, not too much—something that's outside your ordinary expectations but not so far that you come crashing down. Second, it means clearly understanding what you have to do to achieve your goals—what causes will lead to the results you want.

It's important to have specific goals in your practice: That's something many people miss. They think that having a goal means you're constantly depressed about not reaching your goal. Well, that's not how to relate to goals in a skillful way. You set a goal that's realistic but challenging, you figure out what causes, what actions, will get you there, and then you focus on those actions.

You can't practice without a goal, for otherwise everything would fall apart and you yourself would start wondering why you're here, why you're meditating, and why you aren't out sitting on the beach. The trick lies in learning how to relate to your goal in an intelligent way. That's part of the discernment that forms this factor in determination.

Sometimes we're taught not to have goals in the meditation. Usually that's on meditation retreats. You're in a high-pressure environment, you have a limited amount of time, and so you push, push, push. Without any discernment you can do yourself harm. So in a short-term setting like that it's wise not to focus on any particular results you want to brag about after the retreat: "I spent two weeks at that monastery, or one week at that meditation center, and I came back with the first jhana." Like a trophy. You usually end up—if you get something that you can call jhana when you go home—with an unripe mango. You've got a green mango on your tree and someone comes along and says, "A ripe mango is yellow and it's soft." So you squeeze your mango to make it soft and paint it yellow to make it look ripe, but it's not a ripe mango. It's a ruined mango.

A lot of ready-mix jhana is just like that. You read that it's supposed to be like this, composed of this factor and that, and so you add a little of this and a pinch of that, and presto!—there you are: jhana. When you set time limits like that for yourself, you end up with who-knows-what.

Now, when you're not on a retreat, when you're looking at meditation as a daily part of your life, you need to have overall, long-range goals. Otherwise your practice loses focus, and the "practice of daily life" becomes a fancy word for plain old daily life. You need to keep reminding yourself about why you're meditating, about what the meditation really means in the long-term arc of your future. You want true happiness, dependable happiness, the sort of happiness that will stay with you through thick and through thin.

Then, once you're clear about your goal, you have to use discernment both to figure out how to get there and to psyche yourself up for staying on the path you've picked. What this often means is turning your attention from the goal and focusing it on the steps that will take you there. You focus more on what you *do* than on the results you hope to get from what you do. For example, you can't sit here and say, "I'm going to get the first jhana," or the second jhana, or whatever, but you *can* say, "I'm going to stay here and be mindful of every breath for the next whole hour. Each and every one." That's focusing on the causes. Whether or not you reach a particular level of jhana lies in the area of results. Without the causes, the results won't come, so discernment focuses on the causes and lets the causes take care of the results.

The next element—once you've decided on your goal and how you're going to approach it—is to stay true to that determination. In other words, you really stick to your vow and don't suddenly change your mind in mid-course. The only good reason for changing your mind would be if you find that you're doing serious damage to yourself. Then you might want to reconsider the situation. Otherwise, if it's just an inconvenience, or a hardship, you stick with your determination no matter what.

This is your way of learning how to trust yourself. Truthfulness, *"sacca,"* is not simply a matter of speaking the truth. It also means sticking truly to what you've made up your mind to do. If you don't stick truly to that, you've become a traitor to yourself. And when you can't rely on yourself, who *will* you rely on? You go hoping for someone else to rely on, but they can't do the work you have to do. So you learn to be true to your determination.

The third element in a good determination is relinquishment. In other words, while you're being true to your determination there are things you're going to have to give up. There's a verse in the *Dhammapada:* "If you see a greater happiness that comes from forsaking a lesser happiness, be willing to forsake the lesser happiness for the sake of the greater one."

A famous Pali scholar once insisted that that couldn't possibly be the meaning of the verse because it was so obvious. But if you look at people's lives, it's not obvious at all. Many times they give up long-term happiness for a quick fix. If you take the easy way out for a day, then you take the easy way out for the next day and the next, and your long-term goal just never materializes. The momentum never builds up.

The things that really pull you off the path are those that look good and promise a quicker gratification. But once you've got the results of the quick fix, many times you don't get any gratification at all—it was all an illusion. Or you get a little bit, but it wasn't worth it.

That's one of the reasons why the Buddha presents those strong images for the drawbacks of sensual pleasure. A drop of honey on a knife blade. A burning torch you're holding in front of you, upwind, as you're running. A little piece of flesh that a small bird has in its claws, while other, bigger birds are coming to steal it, and they're willing to kill the smaller bird if they don't get it.

These are pretty harsh images but they're harsh on purpose, for when the mind gets fixated on a sensual pleasure it doesn't want to listen to anybody. It's not going to be swayed by soft, gentle images. You have to keep reminding yourself in strong terms that if you really look at sensual pleasures, there's nothing much: no true gratification and a lot of true danger.

I once had a dream that depicted the sensual realm as nothing more than two types of people: dreamers and criminals. Some people sit around dreaming about what they'd like, while others decide that they won't take No for an answer, they're going to get what they want even if they have to get violent. It's a very unpleasant world to be in. That's the way the sensual realm really is, but we tend to forget because we're so wrapped up in our dreams, wrapped up in our desires, that we don't look at the reality of what we do in the process of our dreaming, what we do in the process of trying to get what we want.

So learn to reflect often on these things. This is one of the reasons why your determination should start out with discernment. You have to use discernment all the way along the path to remind yourself that the lesser pleasures really are lesser. They're not worth the effort and especially not worth what you're giving up in terms of a larger pleasure, a larger happiness, a larger wellbeing.

The fourth and final element in a proper determination is peace. You try to keep the mind calm in the course of working toward your goal. Don't get worked up over the difficulties, don't get worked up over the things you're having to give up, don't get worked up about how much time you've already spent on the path and how much remains to be covered. Focus calmly on the step right ahead of you and try to keep an even temper throughout.

The second meaning of peace here is that once you've reached the goal there should be a steady element of calm. If you've reached the goal and the mind is still all stirred up, it's a sign that you chose the wrong goal. There should be a deeper pacification, a deeper calmness that sets in once you've attained the goal.

As the Buddha said, it's normal that while you're working toward a goal there's going to be certain amount of dissatisfaction. You want something but you're not there yet. Some people advise that, in order to get rid of that dissatisfaction, you should just lower your standards. Don't have goals. But that's really selling yourself short, and it's a very unskillful way of getting rid of that sense of dissatisfaction. The skillful way is to do what has to be done, step by step, to arrive at the goal, to get what you want. Then the dissatisfaction is replaced, if it's a proper goal, by peace.

So, as you look at the goals in your meditation, in your life, try to keep these four qualities in mind: discernment, truthfulness, relinquishment, and peace. Be discerning in your choice of a goal and the path that you're going to follow to get there. Once you've made up your mind that it's a wise goal, be true to your determination; don't be a traitor to it. Be willing to give up the lesser pleasures that get in the way, and try to keep your mind on an even keel as you work toward your goal. That way you find that you stretch yourself—not to the point of breaking, but in ways that allow you to grow.

As you learn to push yourself a little bit more, a little bit more, a little bit more than you thought possible, you find that each little bit becomes quite a lot. It all adds up, and you find that the practice can take you to places that you otherwise wouldn't have imagined.

The Dignity of Restraint

September, 2001

It's always interesting to notice which words disappear from common usage. We have them in our passive vocabulary, we all know their meaning, but they tend to disappear from day-to-day conversation—which usually means that they've disappeared from the way we shape our lives. Several years back I gave a Dhamma talk in which I happened to mention the word "dignity." After the talk, a woman in the audience who had emigrated from Russia came to me and said that she had never heard Americans use the word "dignity" before. She had learned it when she studied English over in Russia, but she never heard people use it here. And it's good to think about why. Where and why did it disappear?

I think the reason is related to another word that tends to disappear from common usage, and that's "restraint": foregoing certain pleasures, not because we have to, but because they go against our principles. The opportunity to indulge in those pleasures may be there, but we learn how to say No. This of course is related to another word we tend not to use, and that's "temptation." Even though we don't have to believe that there's someone out there actively tempting us, there are things all around us that do, that tempt us to give in to our desires. And an important part of our practice is that we exercise restraint. As the Buddha says, restraint over the eyes, ears, nose, tongue, and body is good, as is restraint in terms of our actions, our speech, and our thoughts.

What's good about it? Well, for one thing, if we don't have any restraint, we don't have any control over where our lives are going. Anything that comes across our way immediately pulls us in its wake. We don't have any strong sense of priorities, of what's really worthwhile, of what's not worthwhile, of the pleasures we'd gain by saying No to other pleasures. How do we rank the pleasures in our lives, the happiness, the sense of wellbeing that we get in various ways? Actually, there's a sense of wellbeing that comes from being totally independent, from not needing other things. If that state of wellbeing doesn't have a chance to develop, if we're constantly giving in to our impulse to do this, our desire to do that, we'll never know what that wellbeing is.

At the same time, we'll never know our impulses. When you simply ride with your impulses, you don't understand their force. They're like the currents below the surface of a river: Only if you try to build a dam across the river will you become acquainted with those currents and appreciate how strong they are. So we have to look at what's important in life, develop a strong sense of priorities, and be willing to say No to the currents that would lead to less worthwhile pleasures. As the Buddha said, if you see a greater pleasure that comes from forsaking a lesser pleasure, well, be willing to forsake that lesser pleasure for the sake of the greater one.

Sounds like a no-brainer, but if you look at the way most people live, they don't think in those terms. They want everything that comes their way. They want to have their cake and enlightenment too, to win at chess without sacrificing a single pawn. Even when they meditate, their purpose in practicing mindfulness is to use it to provide an even more intense appreciation of the experience of every moment in life. That's something you never see in the Buddha's teachings, though. His theme is always that you have to let go of this in order to gain that, give this up in order to arrive at that. There's always a trade-off.

So we're not practicing for a more intense appreciation of scents, sounds tastes, smells, tactile sensations. We're practicing to realize that the mind doesn't need to depend on those things, and that it's healthier without that dependency. Even though the body requires a certain amount of the requisites of food, clothing, shelter, and medicine, there's an awful lot that it doesn't need. And because our use of the requisites involves suffering, both for ourselves and for everyone else involved in their production, we owe it to ourselves and to others to push the envelope in the direction of restraint, to give up the things we don't need, so as to be as unburdensome as possible.

This is why so much of the training lies in learning to put this aside, put that aside, give this up, give that up. Developing this habit makes us reflect: What are the other things in the mind that we haven't yet given up, in terms of our attachments to this, our attachments to that? Could our mind survive perfectly well without those things that we tend to crave? The Buddha's answer is Yes. In fact, it's better off that way.

Still, a very strong part of our mind resists that teaching. We may give up things for a certain while, but the attitude is often, "I gave up this for a certain while, I gave up that for so long, now I can get back to it." That's a typical pattern. Like with the Rains retreat that's winding down right now: People tend to make a lot of vows—"Well, I'll give up cigarettes for the Rains, I'll give up newspapers for the Rains"—but as soon as the Rains is over they go back to their old ways. They've missed the whole point, which is that if you can survive for three months without those things, you can probably survive for the rest of the year without them as well. Hopefully during those three months you've seen the advantages of giving them up. So you can decide, "Okay, I'm going to continue giving them up." Even though you may have the opportunity to say Yes to your desires, you remind yourself to say No.

This principle of restraint, of giving things up, applies to every step of the path. When you're practicing generosity you have to give up things that you might enjoy. You realize the benefits that come from saying No to your desires and allowing other people to enjoy what you're giving away. For example, when you're living in a group there's food to be shared by all. If you give up some of your share so others can enjoy a bigger share, you're creating a better atmosphere in the group. So you have to ask yourself, "Is the sense of satisfaction I get from taking this thing worth the trade?" And you begin to see the advantages of giving up on this level. This is where dignity begins to come back into our lives: We're not just digestive tracts. We're not slaves to our desires. We're their masters.

The same with the precepts: There may be things that you'd like to do and like to say, but you don't do them, you don't say them. Even if you feel that you might get ahead or gain some advantage by saying them, you don't say them because they go against your principles. You find that you don't stoop to the activities that you used to, and there's a sense of honor, a sense of dignity that comes with that: that you can't be bought off with those particular pleasures, with the temptation to take the easy way out. At the same time, you're showing respect for the dignity, the worth, of those around you. And again, this gives dignity to our lives.

When you're meditating, the same process holds. People sometimes wonder why they can't get their minds to concentrate. It's because they're not willing to give up other interests, even for the time being. A thought comes and you just go right after it without checking to see where it's going. This idea comes, that sounds interesting, that looks intriguing, you've got a whole hour to think about whatever you want. If you have that attitude toward the meditation time, nothing's going to get accomplished.

You have to realize that this is your opportunity to get the mind stable and still. In order to do that, you have to give up all kinds of other thoughts: thoughts about the past, thoughts about the future, figuring this out, planning for that, whatever. You have to put them all aside. No matter how wonderful or sophisticated they may be, you just say No to them.

Now if you've been practicing generosity and have really been serious about practicing the precepts, you've developed that habit of being able to say No, which is why generosity and the precepts are not optional parts of the practice. They're your foundation for the meditation. When you've made a practice of generosity and virtue, the mind's ability to say No to its impulses has been strengthened and given finesse. You've seen the good results that come from being able to restrain yourself in terms of your words and deeds. You've seen that restraint means the opposite of deprivation. Now, as you meditate, you've got the opportunity to restrain your thoughts and see what good comes from that. If you really are able to say No to your thoughts, you find that the mind can settle down with a much greater sense of satisfaction in its state of concentration than could possibly come with those ideas, no matter how fantastic they are.

You find that the satisfaction of giving in to those distractions just slips through your fingers as if it were never there. It's like trying to grab a handful of water or a fistful of air. But the sense of wellbeing that comes with being able to repeatedly bring your mind to a state of stillness, even if you haven't gone all the way, begins to permeate everything else in your life. You find that the mind really is a more independent thing than you imagined it could be. It doesn't need to give in to those impulses. It can say No to itself.

And it's even more independent when you develop the discernment that's able to dig out the source of those impulses to see where they come from, to the point where the whole issue of temptation is no longer an issue because there's nothing tempting. You look at the things that would pull the mind out of its stillness, out of its independence, and you realize they're just not worth it. In the past you were training the mind in a sense of hunger—that's what we do when we keep giving in to impulses: We're training ourselves in hunger. But now you train the mind in the other direction and you realize that the sense of hunger you used to cultivate is really a major source of suffering. You're much better off without it.

It's important that we realize the role that restraint plays in overcoming the problem of suffering and finding true wellbeing for ourselves. You realize that you're not giving up anything you really need. You're a lot better off without it. There's a part of the mind that resists this, and our culture hasn't been very helpful at all because it encourages that resistance: "Give in to this impulse, give in to that impulse, obey your thirst. It's good for the economy, it's good for you spiritually. Watch out, if you repress your desires you're going to get tied in all kinds of psychological knots." The lessons that our culture teaches us—to go out and buy, buy, buy, give in, give in—are all over the place. And what kind of dignity comes from following those messages? The dignity of fish gobbling down bait. We've got to unlearn those habits, unlearn those messages, if we want to revive words like dignity and restraint, and to reap the rewards that the reality of dignity and restraint has to offer our minds.

Fears

April, 2003

We're afraid of so many things. There's so much fear in our lives. And yet the texts don't treat fear all that much, largely because there are many different kinds of fear—fear associated with greed, fear associated with anger, fear associated with delusion—and the texts focus more on the emotions behind the fears than on the fears themselves. The implication here is that if you want to understand your fears, you have to understand the emotions behind them. You have to analyze fear not as a single, solid thing, but as a compound of many different factors, to see which part of the fear is dependent on the greed or passion, which part is dependent on the aversion, and which part is dependent on the delusion. Then, when you've taken care of the underlying emotions, you've taken care of the fear.

If there's greed for something, or passion for something, there's the fear that you're not going to get it, or the fear that once you have got it you're going to be deprived of it.

Then there's fear based on anger. You know that if a certain thing happens it's going to hurt, you're going to suffer. You're averse to it, so you're afraid of it.

And then there's the whole area of delusion, of what you don't know, of the great unknown out there. Fear based on delusion can range anywhere from fear of a ghost in the next room, or a strange person in this room, to general existential angst: a sense that something is required of you and you don't know what it is. Human experience seems like such a huge void, something very alien. There's the big sense of fear that there may not be any meaning or purpose to life, that it's just pointless suffering.

So you have to divide out the different kinds of fear, because you need to work not so much on the fear as on its root. Unless you dig down to the different factors, you won't know what kind of fear it is. You won't be able to get to its root causes.

Now, fear is complicated by the fact that it's such a physical emotion. When fear arises it causes all kinds of reactions in the body. The heartbeat speeds up, the stomach juices get churning, and we often confuse the physical reactions for the mental state. In other words, a single flash of fear floods the mind and then recedes, but it sets into motion a huge series of physical reactions that sometimes will take a long time to settle down. And because they don't settle down right away, there's a sense that "I must still be afraid because here are all the physical symptoms of fear." So the first thing in dealing with fear, especially strong fear like this, is to separate the mental state from the physical state.

Some people say they have no trouble reasoning themselves out of the fear, but find that they're still afraid. That may be based on a misunderstanding, on mistaking the physical symptoms of fear for the actual mental state. We have to separate the physical side of the fear from the mental state, because if you're reasoning through the issue, the actual fear itself may be at bay. What seems to live on, or seems to be unwilling to go away, is the physical side, and of course it takes a while to go away because of the hormones churned up in your blood stream. It's going to take a while for them to wash out.

So your first line of defense is to learn to know when there actually is fear in the mind and when there's no fear in the mind, even though there may be the signs of fear in the body. When you can make this distinction, you don't feel so overwhelmed by the emotion. You breathe as best you can through the physical manifestations of fear, the tension, the feelings that come with that shortened breath or the constricted breath that result from the fear. Then consciously expand that sensation of physical relief and open it up to counteract the fear's physical symptoms.

At the same time, ask yourself, "Exactly what is this fear?" "What's being threatened?" "Where do you feel weak?" "What is the danger?" Learn to take the reasons for the fear apart, because a lot of the fear lies in the confusion. You don't know exactly what you're afraid of, or you don't know exactly what to do. All the avenues seem closed and you can't analyze what's going on. And that multiplies the fear.

So you have to sit down, if you have the chance to sit down, or at least mentally make a note: "What is this fear? Exactly what sparked it?" Learn to look at the fear not as something that *you're* feeling but something that's simply there. And try to look at *why* it keeps shouting at you over and over and over in the brain.

Some fears are neurotic. They're based on gross delusion and they're relatively easy to deal with. Those are the ones that psychotherapists can handle. You had a really bad experience as a child and you've instinctively been avoiding that particular issue, that particular feeling, ever since, but it's gotten to the point where it's totally unrealistic. And because the fear is unrealistic, the treatment is to simply look at the situation for what it really is. You confront it, you try not to avoid it, but actually put yourself into circumstances that will bring up that fear again and watch the disjunction between the fear and the reality. You learn that the reality was not as bad as you thought it would be. As this disjunction grows clearer, the fear gets calmer, weaker, more and more manageable. That's how you handle neurotic fear.

Realistic fears require deeper practice. One of the members of our community lost her mother in a war, came to the States, and became a psychotherapist. As part of her training she had to undergo psychotherapy. After a couple of years of psychotherapy, the therapist said, "It looks like your fears are very realistic. There's nothing I can do for you." This is where Dhamma practice comes in: facing our realistic fears, our fears of aging, illness, separation, and death. These things are real and they do cause suffering—if you don't work your way down into exactly where your attachments are. This is precisely the Buddhist take on fear: It comes from clinging and attachment. And the clinging is threatened by impermanence, by stress and suffering, by the fact that these things are beyond your control. The purpose of our training here is to learn how not to let our happiness be based on things beyond our control, because as long as we entrust our happiness to them, we're setting ourselves up for suffering, setting ourselves up for fear.

This is how the meditation in and of itself is a way of dealing with the fears—the deeper fears, the realistic fears. Ask yourself, "What exactly does my happiness depend on?" Normally, people will allow their happiness to depend on a whole lot of conditions. And the more you think about those conditions, the more you realize that they're totally beyond your control: the economy, the climate, the political situation, the continued beating of certain hearts, the stability of the ground beneath your feet, all of which are very uncertain. So what do you do? You learn to look inside. Try to create a sense of wellbeing that can come simply with being with the breath. Even though this isn't the total cure, it's the path toward the cure. You learn to develop a happiness less and less dependent on things outside, and more and more inward, something more under your control, something you can manage better. And as you work on this happiness you find that it's not a second best. It actually is better than the kind of happiness that was dependent on things outside. It's much more gratifying, more stable. It permeates much more deeply into the mind.

In fact, it allows the mind to open up, because for most of us the mind jumps around like a cat. Wherever it lands, it's always going to stay tense, for it knows it has to be ready to jump again at any moment. But when you find something you can stay with for long periods of time, the mind can allow itself to relax. When it knows that it won't have to jump anytime soon, it can soften up a bit. When it softens up you find it easier to know the mind in and of itself: what it's like, where its attachments are, where it's still clinging. That allows you to go deeper still.

And we find that our ultimate fear is fear of death, which is an extremely realistic fear. It's going to happen for sure, and for most of us it's a huge mystery. This is where the solution has to lie in the meditation, for only meditation can take you to something beyond death, beyond space and time. Death is something that happens within space and time, but there is something that can be experienced outside of those dimensions. That's what we're looking for.

As the texts say, there are four reasons why people fear death. One, they're attached to their bodies—they know they're going to lose their bodies at death. Two, they're attached to sensory pleasures—they know they're going to lose them at death. These two types of fear are based on passion: passion for the body, passion for our sensual appetites. The third type of fear is based on aversion, when people know that they have done cruel things in the past and that they may have to face punishment for those cruel things after death. The fourth type of fear is based on delusion, when people are uncertain about the true Dhamma: "Was the Buddha right? Is there really a Deathless?" As long as you don't know these things directly for yourself, there's always going to be an uncertainty, a large amount of ignorance and delusion surrounding death, creating fear.

The whole purpose of the practice is to counteract these causes for fear, so that you aren't dependent on the body, you don't have to cling to the body for your happiness, you don't have to cling to sensory pleasures for your happiness, you train yourself to do good things, and you reach the point where you taste the Deathless and know for sure that you're on the right path to the right goal.

To do this you have to take apart the basic building blocks of experience, as you encounter them in concentration: form, feeling, perceptions, thought-fabrications, and consciousness. You look to see where these things are inconstant. Where they're inconstant, you realize they're stressful. There's stress right there in the inconstancy. Then when you look at stress, look at suffering—although at this level it's more stress than suffering—you ask yourself, "What am I doing to cause that stress, to aggravate that stress? What activities are accompanying the stress?" You look for the cause, and it's right there in your intentional actions.

When you can take those intentions apart, things open up. Once they open up, you realize that you've come to something totally different, a totally different dimension, outside of space and time. And you realize that death can't touch that. Only with that direct experience can you say that you've overcome your fear of death. The only fear you're left with is the fear you might have lapses of mindfulness where you might do something unskillful. So there is still work to be done. At the very least, though, in the gross sense of the five precepts, you wouldn't intentionally do anything unskillful.

So this is how the meditation deals with fear. It breaks the fear down into other emotions, looking for the underlying causes in terms of the greed, passion, anger, and delusion that give rise to the fear and keep it going. At the same time, the meditation points directly at the way we pin our hopes for happiness on undependable things, and opens the way for us to pin our hopes, not on something changeable or out of our control, but on a dimension beyond the reach of things that could harm it. So the cure for fear is not just a matter of talking yourself out of it, but of putting yourself in a position of strength, where there really is no danger, nothing to fear.

So these are a few thoughts on dealing with the emotion of fear as it comes.

—Learn to separate the physical from the mental side, so you don't misunderstand what's happening in the body, so it doesn't stir up more confusion in the mind.

—Learn how to focus directly on the mind, to see exactly what the problem is, where the sense of weakness is, where the clinging is, because wherever there's clinging there's weakness. And that's what constitutes fear.

—Then look to see if that danger is realistic. If it's not, there's one way of dealing with it; if it's realistic, there's another deeper way of dealing with it.

This way you find you can not only get a handle on your fear or learn to cope with fear but ultimately put yourself in a position where there truly is nothing to fear. And that's what makes this practice so special. Freud once said that the purpose of psychotherapy is to take people out of their neurotic suffering and leave them with the ordinary miseries of daily life. The Dhamma, however, takes you from the ordinary miseries of human life and leads you beyond, to a dimension where there is no misery, no suffering, at all. It deals not only with unrealistic fears or fears that are way out of proportion, but also with the fears that are genuinely realistic and well founded. It can take you beyond even those to a point where, in all reality, there is nothing to fear.

Skills to Take with You

November 12, 1996

When we come out to the monastery like this, we come to a place cut off from human society—not totally cut off, because there are other human beings here, but it's a different kind of society: a society where the bottom line is the practice, the growth of the mind, the growth of the heart, the development of mindfulness, concentration, and discernment. That's not the bottom line in the world at large, but it is the bottom line here, because the mind needs this kind of environment to develop its best qualities. When we live in the world we tend to pick up the values of the world—and what do those values say? They say it doesn't matter what you do as long as you succeed, as long as you get ahead, as long as you get money. That's the important thing. People try to dress these values up to sound a little better than that, but that's basically what they come down to. And when you live with people who hold to these values and you don't have a good solid basis within yourself to withstand that kind of thinking, you've got to give in. You tend to follow along with them whether you like it or not.

But the Buddha teaches us that true happiness isn't found that way. He says that true happiness comes from developing good qualities in the mind. It has nothing to do with money, nothing to do with status, nothing to do with the opinions of other people. It's something totally inner, and it has to come from inner goodness. This is revolutionary, because the world tells you if you want to get ahead you have to develop all sorts of qualities you can't really be proud of: the qualities you need to stab people in the back, make a quick buck, take advantage of other peoples' weaknesses. But the Buddha says that true happiness requires you to develop things like persistence, perseverance, endurance, integrity, mindfulness, kindness, reliability.

These are things you can be proud to develop. There's a dignity to the practice that you don't find in the world outside. But if you're living in a worldly environment, what the Buddha says sounds like a dream, lots of nice ideas but not all that realistic. That's why you need places like this where the values that the Buddha teaches are realistic. It's what life here at the monastery is all about.

So being here gives the mind a chance to develop these qualities and to see that they really do lead to happiness. They really are important, much more so than the things the world holds to be important. This is why physical seclusion is so essential. You get in touch with yourself out here. You get in touch with what's really important in your life. The issues of birth, aging, illness, and death become very large out here. In the world—the ordinary world—these issues get shunted aside. People don't have time for them, and so when aging, illness, and death *do* hit, it's like a big surprise. The mind isn't prepared. People get blown away even though everyone knows, deep down inside, that these things have to happen. Yet when you live in a society that doesn't give you time to look at these things, to reflect on them, and to prepare for them, you really get knocked to pieces when they come. So you need a chance to get out and look at what's really important in your life and how you're going to prepare for these things.

That's what the meditation is all about—developing a good solid basis in the mind that can withstand these things when they come. The image the Buddha gives for this basis is of a stone column, eight cubits long. Four cubits are buried down in the ground in a good solid mountain. Four cubits are above ground. When the wind comes, the column doesn't shake at all. It doesn't even shiver. No matter how strong the wind, no matter which direction it's coming from, the stone column stays put. That's the kind of mental state you need in order to withstand these things—and that's what you develop in the course of the meditation.

Then, as we all know, it's important that you don't cultivate this skill only while you're here, this place of physical solitude, but that you also take this skill back with you. Many times people come to the monastery and say that it's such a relief for the mind to be out here and they'd like to take that state of mind with them when they go back. Well, you can't take a state of mind like that with you. It's a result. What you can take back is the skill, the cause of that state of mind. It's not just the environment that allows it to develop. People can come out here and still have their minds a total mess. What makes the difference is that you learn how to make use of the environment to develop the skills you need to straighten out things inside. The skills are the things you *can* take back with you when you go home—the skillful attitudes, the skillful approaches to bringing the mind under control, giving it a sense of stability inside. These are the important parts of the practice that train the mind to stand on its own two feet.

When you ask yourself, "Where is the best place to meditate?", your answer should be, "Right here, wherever you are. That's the best place." That's the ideal. But as you're getting started, you're like a child learning to ride a bicycle—you need training wheels, you need help. You can't just jump on the bicycle and ride off with a perfect sense of balance. You use the training wheels, you use the community, you use the peaceful environment to help get the mind in the proper attitude. Then you try to develop your own skills so that when the training wheels are taken away, you can ride with ease and won't fall over.

What are some of these skills? The most basic one is just learning to focus the mind on one thing and to withstand any temptation to let it go. This is an important skill you need whatever your work is. If you can concentrate on your work and don't let the distractions get in your way, work gets done and it gets done properly. It's a solid piece of work, and not just little bits and pieces that happen to be thrown together, because there's a continuity. And when you learn how to focus on one thing like this, when you focus in on the breath, it changes your attitude toward the other thoughts that come into the mind. If the mind doesn't have a particular focus, it can wander around from thought to thought, not really noticing what it's doing, and not having a sense of direction.

It gets lost going in the wrong direction, because every direction is just the direction where it's flowing.

But when you give it something to hold onto, you have a sense of direction. Then you can see how some things pull you away and some things pull you back. It's like the difference of being on the earth and being out in outer space. When you're on the earth, there's a definite sense of orientation—there's north, south, east, and west. You've got the earth as your reference point. But if you're out in outer space, you don't know which way is up, which way is down, north, south, east, west—they have no meaning out there. And the mind is just adrift in the stellar currents. But when you're on the earth, when you've got a good basis, then you have a sense that, "This way is north, this way is south." You have a sense of the direction you want to go, and you know when you're heading in that direction and when you're not.

That's why it's crucial to have a center for the mind. But to maintain that center, you have to enjoy it. If you don't, it simply becomes one more burden to carry in addition to your other burdens, and the mind will keep dropping it when your other burdens get heavy. This is why we spend so much time working on the skill of playing with the breath, making it comfortable, making it gratifying, making it fill your body with a sense of ease. When you have that kind of inner nourishment to feed on, you're less hungry for things outside. You don't need to feed on the words and actions of other people. You don't have to look for your happiness there. When you can develop a sense of inner fullness simply by the way you breathe, the mind can stay nourished no matter what the situation. You can sit in a boring meeting and yet be blissing out—and nobody else has to know. You can watch all the good and bad events around you with a sense of detachment because you have no need to feed on them. It's not that you're indifferent or apathetic, simply that your happiness doesn't have to go up and down with the ups and downs of your life. You're not in a position where people can manipulate you, for you're not trying to feed on what they have to offer you. You've got your own source of food inside.

At the same time, when you have an inner center like this to hold onto, you develop a sense of dissociation from the thoughts that arise within the mind. You realize—when you're focused on the breath and a thought comes into the mind—it's not necessarily *you* thinking or *your* thought, and you're not necessarily responsible for it. You don't have to follow it and check it out or straighten it out. If it comes in half-formed, just let it go away half-formed. You don't have to be responsible for it.

This is another important skill, because if you can learn to step back from the thoughts and emotions that come into the mind and not say that this is *my* thought or this is *my* emotion, then you can really choose which ones are worth holding onto, which ones should be explored, and which ones should be let go, that you don't have to deal with at all. Some people may say that that's irresponsible, that you've got to check everything out. "Well, that's just what they say. What do they know?": That's the kind of attitude you have to develop.

As the Buddha said, his own practice really got started in the right direction when he divided his thoughts into two types: skillful and unskillful. What this means is having the ability to step back from your thoughts and look at them not in terms of their content, but in terms of where they take you. If you have thoughts motivated by greed, anger, delusion, passion, aversion, confusion, boredom—where do they take you? Well, they don't take you to nibbana, that's for sure. They don't take you where you want to go, so you decide to dissociate from them. You don't deny that they exist, for that would just drive them underground. You admit their existence but you realize that you don't have to follow them. You can let them go, and they pass away from the mind. Meanwhile, you latch onto more skillful thinking—either that, or you learn how to let go of thoughts and just keep the mind still where it doesn't have to think. This is where you gain a sense that you're more in control of your mind, that you're not subject to everything that comes passing through.

Most people's minds are like bus stations. Everyone who wants to go through the bus station has the right to do so. And they can do all kinds of weird things while they're there in the bus station: mugging people, having sex in the restroom stalls, shooting up heroin back in the dark corners. That's what most peoples' minds are like. You've got to make up your mind to turn your mind into a home, a place where you have the right to let thoughts in or not let them in, as you like—or let them just go passing on. You can close the windows and doors and let in only your friends. You're more in control. And when you have a home like that, you can settle down and be at ease and at peace at home, at ease and at peace with your own mind. So this is an important skill to take with you wherever you go. It's not a skill that you use only while you're sitting here with your eyes closed.

One of the essential techniques you need in this skill is the ability to breathe through your thoughts, because when thoughts come heavy—when they come really strong—they don't just affect the mind. They affect the body as well. That's why when anger comes you have a strong sense that you have to get it out of your system because it's gotten into the body, into the way you breathe, into the patterns of tension in the body. It builds up and gets hard to bear, so you feel you've got to get it out. Most people think that the way to get it out is to say something or do something under the power of the anger, but that doesn't solve anything at all. When we're with our breathing practice, we learn how breathe through that pattern of tension in the chest or the belly and let it disperse throughout the body. Once it's dispersed it loses its power. You feel less oppressed by it. Then you can look at the situation from a calm vantage point and decide what should be done. Do you have to say something? Is this the best time to say it, or is it best left unsaid? How will people react if you talk now? Should you wait till a later time? You can gauge these things clearly, which you can't do when you've got a sense of weightiness or oppression from the anger inside the body. So you breathe through the patterns of tension in the body. It's an important skill you use not only while you're here, but also while you're out working, while you're dealing with your family, whatever you're doing in the world at large.

It's important to realize that the skills of meditation are for use not only while you're on the cushion or sitting with your legs crossed and your eyes closed. They're basic skills for governing your own mind, looking after your own mind, administering the ways your mind works, whether you're sitting with your eyes closed or open, whether you're alone or dealing with people, because it's the same mind. The defilements that arise in the course of your practice and the defilements that arise in the course of daily life are basically the same defilements. Sometimes in society the defilements appear more unexpectedly, with more force and a greater sense of urgency, but they come down to the same thing— if an unskillful state arises in the mind and you treat it unskillfully, then you just go wherever it leads you. But if you learn how to deal skillfully even with the unskillful things that come—to deal skillfully with feelings of passion, feelings of anger, your own misunderstandings—you can take the raw material of life and turn it into something fine.

As Ajaan Lee once said, "A person with intelligence takes whatever gets sent his or her way and makes something good out of it." This is the attitude you've got to adopt because we live a life full of the power of kamma—old kamma and new. You can't do anything about old kamma. You have to accept it like a good sport. That's why you practice equanimity. But as for the new kamma you're creating right now, you can't practice equanimity with that. You have to be very concerned about what you're putting into the system because you realize that this is the only chance you get to make the choice. Once the choice is made and it gets put into the system, then whatever the energy—positive or negative—that's the sort of energy you're going to have to experience.

So pay attention: What are you putting into the system right now? This is the important thing to focus on. Whatever other people do to you, whatever arises in your body in terms of pains, illnesses, aging, death, or whatever: That's old kamma that you simply have to learn to take with good humor, with a sense of equanimity. As for what you're putting into the system right now, that's serious business. That's where your attention and efforts should be focused.

So the skills you pick up from the Buddha's teachings are not just techniques for silent meditation. They're skillful attitudes, skillful approaches you develop to what's important in life. You want to approach life as a skill, to realize that there is always the possibility of doing things skillfully. You may not have perfected it, but you don't beat yourself for not having the perfect response to every situation. You realize that there's always the opportunity to learn. You make mistakes, you learn from them. This is a normal part of life, and a wise way of living is to learn from your mistakes and resolve not to repeat them. Learn from what you've done. Notice when you do things correctly, notice when you make mistakes, and take that information to adjust your patterns of behavior.

Some people come to the practice and say, "Well, this is the kind of person I am. I've just got to be this way." That attitude closes the door on the practice entirely. You start from where you are, but you have to be willing to change. If people couldn't change, if they had to stay the way they are, the Buddha's teaching would be in vain. There would be no reason to have the teachings because they're all about transformation. They're all about learning, developing, changing the way you approach life. From the Buddhist point of view, "accepting yourself" means not only admitting where you are, but also accepting that you have the potential to change. As your approach becomes more and more skillful, you're doing less and less harm to yourself, less harm to others, less harm to both. You find that you live in a way that brings more benefits for yourself, more benefits for others, more benefits for both. It may take more energy, more attention, but it's a much more worthwhile way of living.

It's like being an expert carpenter. You've got various ways of approaching the problems that arise in the mind. You realize that there are all kinds of problems and there are many ways of dealing with them. If you try just one approach, it's like having a tool box full of nothing but saws. You can't build anything with that. You can't be called a decent carpenter at all. But when you realize that there are ways of dealing with different situations that arise, and, through your own powers of observation, you discover which ways work for you, which ways get the right results for you: That's called having a full tool box, with a wide range of tools. And when you have those tools at hand, you can stay anywhere. You can stay in a monastery, you can stay in a hospital, you can stay at work, at home, in this country, in another country, this world, the next world, this life, the next. The tools stay with you once you've developed them.

So focus on the practice as a way of collecting tools, developing skills, both in terms of techniques in the meditation and in terms of whole attitudes toward your life. That's the most worthwhile use of your time. Those are the best things to take with you when you go.

Maintenance Work

December, 2002

Get your body into position. Sit straight, hands on your lap. Close your eyes.

Get your mind in position. Think about the breath and be aware of the sensation of the breathing.

See? It's not all that hard. Just *doing* it is not the hard part. The hard part is the maintaining: keeping it there. That's because the mind isn't used to staying in position, just as the body isn't used to staying in position. But the mind tends to move a lot faster and to be a lot more fickle than the body, which is why we have to work extra hard at that really hard aspect of the training: keeping the mind in one place, maintaining it in concentration.

Ajaan Lee once said there are three steps in concentration practice: doing, maintaining, and then using the concentration. The using is fun. Once the mind has settled down, you can use it as a basis for understanding things. You suddenly see the motions of the mind as it creates thoughts, and it's a fascinating process to watch, to take apart.

The maintaining, though, isn't all that fascinating. You learn a lot of good lessons about the mind in the course of maintaining, and without those lessons you couldn't do the more refined work of gaining insight. But still, it's the most difficult part of the practice. Ajaan Lee once compared it to putting a bridge across a river. The pilings on this bank and that bank aren't hard to place, but the pilings in the middle are really hard. You've got to withstand the current of the river. You dig down and put a few stones on the bottom of the river and you come back with your next load of stones only to discover that the first load of stones has washed away. This is why you need techniques for getting that middle set of pilings to stay in place, for otherwise the bridge will never get across the river at all.

So this is what we work at. In the beginning, the work is simply a question of noticing when the mind has slipped off and bringing it back. When it's slipped off again, you bring it back again. And again. And again. But if you're observant, you become sensitive to the signs that tell you when the mind is about to slip off. It hasn't gone yet but it's getting ready to go. It's tensed up and ready to jump. When you can sense that tension, you simply relax it. Meticulously. And that way you can keep the mind more and more consistently with the breath.

Be especially careful not to ask where the mind was going to jump. You can't give into that temptation. Sometimes the mind is getting ready to jump off to something and you wonder, "Where is it going? Anyplace interesting?" Or when a thought begins to form: It's just a vague, inchoate sense of a thought, and the mind puts a label on it. Then you want to see, "Does this label really fit?" And that means you're fully entangled. If you look more carefully at the process of what's happening, you begin to realize that whether the label fits or not, the mind has a tendency to make it fit. So it's not a question of whether it's a true label or not, but whether you want to follow through with that process of making it fit. And you don't have to. You notice a little stirring in the mind, and you don't have to label it. Or if you've labeled it, you don't have to ask whether the label is true or not. Just let it go. That way the stirring can disband.

Now, when the mind finally *does* settle down, in the beginning there can be a sense of rapture, a sense of accomplishment, that you've finally gotten the mind to stay with the breath for long periods of time, for longer and longer periods of time. It feels really refreshing to be there. Then you make it a game, seeing how quickly you can get there, how often you can get there, what other activities you can be doing at the same time. However—and I don't want to spoil it for you—there comes a time when this gets boring, too.

It's boring, though, only because you lose perspective. Everything seems so calm, everything seems so settled, and there's a part of the mind that gets bored. Oftentimes that's your first object lesson in insight: Look into the boredom. Why is the mind bored with a state of calm and ease? After all, the mind is in its most secure place, its most comfortable place. Why would part of you want to go looking for trouble, to stir things up? Look into that. There's a chance for insight right there.

Or, you start telling yourself, "This is really stupid, just sitting here still, still, calm, calm. This isn't intelligent at all." That's when you have to remind yourself that you're working on a foundation. The stronger the foundation, then when the time comes to build a building, the taller it can go, the more stable it will be. When insights come, you want them to be solid insights. You don't want them to knock you askew. How can insights knock you askew? You gain an insight and get so excited about it that you lose perspective, forget to take it and look on the other side. When an insight comes, Ajaan Lee always recommends turning it inside out. The insight says, "This must be this." Well, he says, try thinking about what if it were *not* this. What if it were the opposite? Would there be a lesson there as well? In other words, just as you're not supposed to fall for the content of your thoughts, you're not supposed to fall for the contents of your insights, either.

That requires really stable concentration, because many times when the insights come they're very striking, very interesting. A strong sense of accomplishment comes with them. To keep yourself from getting carried away by that sense of accomplishment, you want to have your concentration really solid so that it's not impressed. It's not bowled over. It's ready to look at the other side of the insight. This is one reason why you need solid concentration, to work at the steady, steady job of just coming back, staying, staying, keeping it still, keeping it still.

Then that old question of perception begins coming up again. The whole perception of your state of mind starts getting questionable. File that one away for future reference. As the Buddha said, all the states of concentration, all the states of jhana, up through the state of nothingness, are perception-attainments. The perception you apply to them is what keeps them going. And as you stay with a particular level, there starts to be a slight sense of the artificiality of the corresponding perception. But wait until the concentration is really solid before you start questioning it, for the perception is what keeps the state of concentration going—and it *is* an artificial state that you're creating in the mind. When the time comes for insight, one of the topics that you'll want to focus on is the artificiality of that concept, the artificiality of the perception that creates the state of concentration you've been living with. For the time being, though, just file it away for future reference. If you question things too early, everything gets short-circuited, and you're back to where you started.

So even though the work of maintaining concentration may seem like drudgery work—just coming back, coming back, coming back—everything depends on this quality of consistency, of maintenance. Get really good at it, really familiar with it. The more familiar you are with it, the more easily you can use it as the basis for insight when the time comes.

There's a passage where the Buddha talks about a meditator whose mind has attained a really solid stage of equanimity. When you're solid in your equanimity, you realize that you can apply it to different things. You can apply it to the sense of infinite space. You can apply it to the sense of infinite consciousness or nothingness. Once you recognize precisely where those perceptions are, precisely how you can focus on them and stay there for long, long times, you'll suddenly gain insight into how constructed they are.

In the beginning it's very obvious how constructed they are because you're working so hard to put them together. But as you get more and more familiar with them, there's a greater sense that you're simply tuning-in to something already there. You're more impressed by the "already-there-ness" of the state. You begin to overlook the act of tuning-in because it gets easier and easier, more and more natural—but it's still there, the element of construction, the element of fabrication that keeps you there. When the concentration gets really solid so that you can look into it even in its most refined state, that's when the insight really hits you: how constructed this is, how artificial the whole thing is—this state you've learned to depend on. And only then is the insight meaningful.

If you start analyzing states of concentration in terms of the three characteristics before you've really depended on those states, before you've really gotten familiar with them, it short-circuits the whole process. "Oh yes, concentration is unstable." Well, anyone can sit and meditate for two minutes and learn that, and it doesn't mean very much. But if you develop the skill so that you're really solidly with it, you test that principle of inconstancy. How constant can you make this state of the mind? Ultimately, you get to the point where you realize that you've made it as constant as you could ever make it, as reliable as you could ever make it, and yet it still falls under the three characteristics. It's still constructed.

That's when the mind starts tending toward the unconstructed, the unfabricated. If you've brought the mind to still enough a state of equilibrium, you can stop fabricating and things open up. It's not just an intention of saying, "Well, I'm going to put a stop to this." It's a matter of learning how equilibrium happens without any new intention taking its place. That's where the real skill lies. That's why we spend so much time getting the mind into balance, balance, balance, for only in a real state of balance like that can you totally let go.

Some people have the conception that meditation is about getting the mind into a really extreme state where things "break through." Bring it to the total edge of instability and then suddenly you break through to something deeper. That's what they say. But I've yet to find the Buddha describe it that way. For him it's more a question of bringing the mind to a state of balance so that when the time comes to stop fabricating, the mind doesn't tip over in any direction at all. It's right there.

So these qualities of consistency, persistence, stick-to-it-ivedness, training the mind so it can really trust itself, depend on itself, rely on itself in the midst of all the inconstancy in the world: These are the qualities that make all the difference in the meditation.

Sensitivity All the Time

November, 2002

Try to be present throughout the whole breath, each breath, all the way in, all the way out.

We like to think that if we had it all figured out, we wouldn't have to pay so much attention—that if there were some formula we could memorize, that in itself would take care of things so we wouldn't have to put so much effort into the meditation, put so much effort into being present. We'd like just to plug into the formula and let things go on automatic pilot—but that's missing the point. The point is being attentive, paying careful attention, being sensitive, all the time.

This is a quality the Buddha calls *citta*: intentness, attentiveness, really giving yourself fully to what you're doing right now. When you're intent, insight comes not as a formula that allows you to be inattentive, but as a sensitivity to what's going on right now so you can *read* what's happening, continually. In other words, you're trying to strengthen this quality of being attentive, this quality of being present, because when you're really present you don't need all the other formulas. You recognize the signs of what's going on: when the breath is too long, when the breath is too short, when the breath energy in the body is too sluggish, when it's too active. Being attentive is what enables you to notice these things, to be sensitive to them, to read what they're telling you.

So the insights you gain are not necessarily wise sayings that you can write down in little books of wisdom. Insight is a greater and greater sensitivity to what's going on. Don't think that you'd like to have things explained beforehand, or to sit here trying to come up with little rules or memory aids: "Well, when this happens, you should do this; and then, when that happens, you should do that." You're trying to develop the quality of being able to listen, able to read what's happening in the present moment, all the time, so that you won't need those memory aids.

If you're looking for the little formulas or the little nuggets of wisdom that you can wrap up and take home, in hopes that they'll allow you to drop the effort that goes into being so attentive, it's like the old story of the goose laying the golden egg. You get a golden egg and then you kill the goose. That's the end of the eggs. The goose here is the ability to stay attentive, to be present, to be fully engaged in what's happening with the breath. The insights will come on their own—you keep producing, producing, producing the insights—not for the sake of taking home with you, but for the sake of using them right here, right now. You don't have to be afraid that you're not going to remember them for the next time. If you're really attentive, your sensitivity will produce the fresh insights you need next time. It will keep developing, becoming an ability to read things more and more carefully, more and more precisely, so that you won't have to memorize insights from the past. It will keep serving them up, hot and fresh.

Like sailing a boat: When you first get out in the boat and they give you the rudder, it doesn't take long before you flip the boat over because you steer too hard to the right, steer too hard to the left. You don't have a sense of what's just right. But if you pay attention to what you're doing, after a while that sense of "just right" develops. And the next time you get into the boat, it's not that you have to remember any verbal lessons you learned from the last time. The sensitivity is there in you: the ability to read how much pressure you should put on the rudder at this point, ... when this happens, ... when that happens. There's a greater and greater familiarity that comes from being fully attentive.

The same principle applies here. It's not the case that you're going to be fully attentive for five minutes and learn whatever lessons you're going to need for the hour and then just zone out or go on automatic pilot. You have to be as attentive to the first breath as you are to the last breath, as attentive to the last breath as you are to the first, and all the breaths in between. As this quality of attentiveness grows stronger, your sensitivity grows stronger. There's less and less of a conscious effort, but it doesn't mean that you're less present. It's just that you're more skilled at being present, more skilled at being sensitive, ready to learn whatever lessons there are to learn.

Michaelangelo at the age of 87 reportedly said that he was still learning how to sculpt. Well, that should be your attitude as you meditate. There are always things to learn. Even arahants have things to learn. They've learned enough already to overcome their defilements, but they're still learning other things because they're attentive all the time. They're watching what's going on. Their sensitivity has been heightened.

When people talk about the path being identical with the goal, there *is* an element of truth there, in the sense that when you reach the goal you don't throw away all the things you did when you were on the path. The texts say that even arahants practice the four foundations of mindfulness, not because they have anything more to do in terms of uprooting their defilements, but because the practice of mindfulness provides a pleasant abiding in the here and now. It's a good place to be. At the same time, if they have to teach other people, they use the sensitivities they've developed in their meditation and apply them to the process of teaching.

So don't sit here saying, "Well, I'll just stay with the breath until I get the results I want, and then I can stop this effort." You're working with the qualities that are going to take you there and that are going to stay with you once you arrive: the qualities of mindfulness, alertness, discernment—all the good qualities we're working on here. You want to bring them more and more to bear on what you're doing in every situation. They get stronger and stronger, and they give you the sensitivity you need to cut through any defilements you encounter. They give you the sensitivity you need to find more stable states of concentration, to figure out the techniques you need in order to get the mind to settle down when it's obstreperous.

But again, once you've learned those lessons, it's not the case that you can turn off the effort to be sensitive, the effort to be fully engaged. It's just that you learn how to be more and more comfortable being engaged, so that whatever lessons come up, whatever things you have to read within yourself, whatever things you have to listen to within yourself, you're ready to listen. You're alert to the signs that you have to decipher when you read.

So do what you can to keep this goose alive and well so it can keep laying the golden eggs you need. You crack open the golden egg and there's a lesson for you to use right there, right then. You don't have to worry about making a stockpile of golden eggs, because it's a funny kind of gold, like the gold in a fairy tale. You turn around, and a few minutes later it's turned into feathers or straw. But if you're really attentive, the goose is ready to lay another golden egg. So keep nourishing it, tending to it, so that it can keep producing. Use the eggs for their intended purpose and then just let them go. Do your best to keep this mind-state going so that it's ready to lay another egg, to give you more gold all the time.

The Path of Questions

July, 2001

Let the mind settle down comfortably on the breath. Don't push it too hard and don't let it float away. Try to find just the right amount of pressure for staying with the breath. Let there be just that one question in the mind right now: how heavily to focus on the breath. Other questions you can put aside, because most of the other questions you would be focusing on now would simply foster doubt. The questions dealing with the mind and the breath in the present moment: Those are the ones that are relevant because you can answer them by looking right here, right now.

The point of our practice is to gain discernment that leads to liberation, that leads to release. But before we get to that level of discernment we have to train the discernment we have in every level of the practice.

This morning we read a passage by Ajaan Lee in which he talks about how generosity, virtue, and meditation both *depend* upon discernment and *give rise* to discernment. In other words, you have to use your discernment in each of these levels of the practice. It's not that you have to wait until the very end for discernment to land on you. You take the discernment you have; you exercise it; it gets stronger. It's just like exercising your body. If you want a strong body, what do you do? You take the weak body you've got, exercise it, and it turns into a stronger body, step by step by step because you're using it. But that also means learning how to exercise it properly. You don't exercise it too heavily to the point where you pull a tendon or tear a muscle.

So at each level of the practice there are questions you want to ask to foster discernment appropriate to that level of the practice. When you're practicing generosity you have to ask, "What, right now, is just right? How much can I afford? How much is giving too much? In what way is my gift going to be most beneficial, most effective? If I don't have much to give in terms of material things, what else can I give?" The gift of your time and energy, the gift of forgiveness, can sometimes be many times be more useful than the gift of material things.

That's the development of skill, insight, and discernment on the level of generosity. Then, on the level of the precepts, you work up to a higher level. "How am I going to maintain my precepts in difficult situations?" Say, when people ask questions that you know are going to be harmful if you answer them, how are you going to avoid the answer so that you don't lie? Or how are you going to live in your house so that you don't have to kill pests? Once you've laid down the law for yourself—"Okay, these are the principles I'm going to hold to"—you suddenly find yourself with a whole new set of questions. You'll need ingenuity and discernment to answer them. And as you come up with answers using whatever ingenuity you have, you find that your ingenuity and discernment get stronger.

The same principle holds with meditation. Each step in your meditation requires certain questions. You take the questions bit by bit by bit, step by step and you find that the meditation both requires discernment and strengthens discernment as you use it. For instance, when you're focusing on the breath, you ask a simple question: "What kind of breathing feels good right now?" And then you explore. You're free to experiment with the breath, to find out if long breathing feels good, if short breathing feels good, deep breathing, shallow....

There's an element of investigation already even in the simple practice of concentration. It's not that you make the mind really, really still and then, all of a sudden, discernment's going to go off like a flash bulb. There has to be some discernment involved in the process of getting the mind to settle down. As the Buddha said, there's no jhana without discernment, no discernment without jhana. The two have to go together, to help each other along.

Discernment here is learning which things to develop and which to let go. You start out with really simple things. You have to focus on what the breathing is like, what kind of breathing the body needs right now. If your energy level feels low, what kind of breathing will raise the energy level? If you feel too frenetic, what kind of breathing can calm you down? If there are pains in different parts of the body, are you breathing in a way that's actually augmenting or causing those pains?

These are things you can explore. What you're doing is taking your thinking process, the questioning process of the mind, and learning how to use it skillfully. Meditation is not a matter of stopping your thought processes right away. Eventually there does come a point where thinking gets more and more attenuated until you can hardly call it thinking at all. But in the mean time, before you can get there, you have to learn how to use your thinking skillfully, so you apply it to the issue of concentration, apply it to the issue of settling the mind down.

This is a basic principle in a lot of the Buddha's teachings. In order to learn how to let go of something, you've got to learn how to do it skillfully. This principle doesn't apply to sex, but it does apply to a lot of other things. For instance, some texts talk about going beyond precepts and practices in the practice, but before you can go beyond them you have to learn how to maintain your precepts with skill. Some Zen texts talk about letting go of the discriminating mind, but before you let go of the discriminating mind you have to learn how to use it properly. Before learning how to let go of desire, you have to learn how to use your desire properly. Focus it on the causes that will get you where you want to go. The unskillful use of desire means focusing so much on the results you want that you ignore the causes. You want to skip over them. That kind of desire is unskillful. You're not going to get beyond desire by just dropping unskillful desires. You have to learn how to replace unskillful desires with skillful ones, focused on the causes that will take you where you want to go. Then, when you've arrived, the issue of desire falls away.

So right now focus your desire on what will take you to concentration. This means being mindful to keep the breath in mind,
and being alert, watching the breath. A good way to do that is to
ask yourself questions about the breath and how you can relate to
it here in the present moment. If you were to make the next breath
a little bit longer, what would happen? Try it and find out. How
about a little bit shorter, deeper, stronger, more refined? Just ask
those questions of the mind. Don't put a lot of physical pressure
on the breath. Just ask the question and you'll find that simply
asking the question opens up the possibility.

This is called appropriate attention—*yoniso manasikara,* learning
how to ask skillful questions—and it's essential to the whole practice. In fact the first question you're supposed to ask when you go
to meet a new teacher is: "What is skillful? What is not skillful?
What, if I do it, will be for my long-term happiness? What, if I do
it, will be for my long-term suffering?"

You take those questions, usually starting on the level of the precepts or generosity, and work down deeper and deeper into the mind.
That's how the deeper levels of concentration are attained. The discernment that gives rise to liberation comes in as well, by learning
how to ask the question "What's the skillful thing to do now?"

Now, in order to ask those questions from the very refined
levels of the mind, you have to start by asking them from more bla-
tant levels in your daily life. This is why the Buddha's teaching is
not about how soon we can get the experience of Awakening, how
soon we can get the feeling of oneness so we can go on with the
rest of our life. That's not it at all. You have to train your whole
approach to life. "What's the most skillful thing to do right now?
What's the most skillful thing to say? What's the most skillful thing
to think?" Learn how to keep asking these questions, looking for
the answers, learning from your mistakes time and again, so that
you gradually do become more skillful on the outer levels.

You find that that habit begins to take root in your mind. Then,
as you're sitting here meditating, it becomes an automatic question:
"What's the most skillful way to relate to the breath? What's the

most skillful way to relate to the present moment?" You experiment. You test. You come up with answers. And then you test the answers.

So it's a basic process that starts from the outside and works in. Ultimately it leads to the discernment that liberates the mind totally from suffering. That's the point we all want to get to. But it's not a matter of simply sitting here and waiting until it comes. Liberating discernment comes from the process of questioning and probing and looking and getting the mind to settle down and be really still and asking, "Why is there still a disturbance in there? What acts of mind, what decisions are creating that disturbance?" Sometimes the disturbance is on a very subtle level. "What decisions are still getting in the way?" You look and you watch and you have to be very patient.

Ajaan Khamdee, one of the forest ajaans, once made a comparison. He said that meditating is like being a hunter. The hunter goes out in the forest and, on the one hand, has to be very still so he doesn't scare off the rabbits and other animals, but at the same time he has to be very alert. His ears and eyes have to be very sharp. And the hunter can't say "Well, okay, I'm just going to sit here for half an hour and I'll bag my rabbit." He has no idea how long it's going to take but he maintains that attitude of quiet alertness. The same in your meditation: The concentration is what keeps you quiet; that little question is what keeps you alert. And the combination of the two when you get them just right: That will lead to Awakening.

Admirable Friendship

November 13, 2002

Practicing the Dhamma is primarily an issue of looking at yourself, looking at your own thoughts, your own words, your own deeds, seeing what's skillful, seeing what's not. It's not so much an issue of self-improvement as one of action-improvement, word-improvement, and thought-improvement. This is an important distinction, because people in the modern world—*especially* in the modern world—seem to be obsessed with self-image. We've spent our lives bombarded with images, and you can't help but compare your image of yourself to the images of people you see outside you. And for the most part there's no comparison: You're not as strong, as beautiful, as wealthy, as stylish, and so forth. I noticed in Thailand that, as soon as television became rampant, teenagers became very sullen. I think it's largely this issue of people's looking at themselves in comparison to the images broadcast at them. And the whole question of self-image becomes very sensitive, very painful. So when we say that you're looking at yourself, remember you're not looking at your "self." You're looking at your thoughts, words, and deeds. Try to look at them as objectively as possible, get the whole issue of "self" out of the way, and then it becomes a lot easier to make improvements.

The same applies to your dealings with other people. The Buddha said there are two factors that help most in the arising of discernment, that help you most along the path. The foremost internal factor is appropriate attention. The foremost external factor is admirable friendship. And it's important that you reflect on what admirable friendship means, because even though you're supposed to be looking at your own thoughts, words, and deeds, you're also looking at the thoughts, words, and deeds of the people around you. After all, your eyes are fixed in your body so that they point outside. You can't help but see what other people are doing. So the question is how you can make this knowledge most useful to yourself as you practice. And this is where the principle of admirable friendship comes in.

To begin with, it means associating with admirable people, people who have admirable habits, people who have qualities that are worthy of admiration. One list puts these qualities at four: Admirable people have conviction in the principle of kamma, they're virtuous, they're generous, and they're discerning. There's a well-known line from Dogen where he says, "When you walk through the mist, your robe gets wet without your even thinking about it." That's his description of living with a teacher. You pick up the teacher's habits without thinking about it, but that can be a double-edged sword because your teacher can have both good and bad habits, and you need to be careful about which ones you pick up.

So in addition to associating with admirable people, the Buddha says there are two further factors in admirable friendship. One is that you ask these people about issues of conviction, virtue, generosity, discernment. And this doesn't necessarily mean just asking the teacher. You can ask other people in the community who have admirable qualities as well. See what special insights they have on how to develop those qualities. After all, they've obviously got experience, and you'd be wise to pick their brains.

The second factor is that if you see anything in other people worth emulating, you emulate it, you follow it, you bring that quality into your own behavior. So this makes you responsible for your end of admirable friendship, too. You can't sit around simply hoping to soak up the mist, waiting for it to blow your way. *You* have to be active. Remember that passage in the *Dhammapada* about the spoon not knowing the taste of the soup, while the tongue does know the taste.

But again, when looking at people around you, it's important that you get away from your sense of competitiveness, of this person versus that person. You look, not at them, but at their activities. Otherwise you start comparing yourself to the other person: "This person's better than I am. That person's worse than I am." And that brings in questions of conceit, resentment, and competition, which are not really helpful because we're not here to compete with each other. We're here to work on ourselves. So again, look at other people simply in terms of their thoughts, their words, their actions. And see what's an admirable action, what are admirable words, what are admirable ideas, ones you can emulate, ones you can pick up. In this way the fact that we're living together becomes a help to the practice rather than a hindrance.

The same is true when you notice people around you doing things that are not so admirable. Instead of judging the other person, simply judge the actions by their results: that that particular action, that particular way of thinking or speaking is not very skillful, for it obviously leads to this or that undesirable result. And then turn around and look at yourself, at the things you do and say: Are those unskillful words and actions to be found in you? Look at the behavior of other people as a mirror for your own behavior. When you do this, even the difficulties of living in a community become an aid to the practice.

The Buddha designed the monkhood so that monks would have time alone but also have time together. If you spent all of your time alone, you'd probably go crazy. If you spent all of your time together, life would start getting more and more like dorm life all the time. So you have to learn how to balance the two. Learn how to develop your own good qualities on your own and at the same time use the actions and words of other people as mirrors for yourself, to check yourself, to see what out there is worth emulating, to see what out there is clearly unskillful. And then reflect on yourself, "Do I have those admirable qualities? Do I have those unskillful qualities in my thoughts, words and deeds?" If you've got those unskillful qualities, you've got work to do. If you don't have the admirable ones, you've got work to do there as well.

What's interesting is that in both the internal and external factors—both in appropriate attention and in admirable friendship—one of the crucial factors is questioning. In other words, in appropriate attention you learn how to ask yourself questions about your own actions. In admirable friendship you ask the other people you admire about the qualities they embody. If you find someone whose conviction is admirable, you ask that person about conviction. If you find someone whose effort and persistence are admirable, you ask him about persistence. In other words, you take an interest in these things. The things that we ask questions about, those are the things we're interested in, those are the things that direct our practice. And it's the combination of the two, the internal questioning and the external questioning, that gets us pointed in the right direction.

So this is something to think about as you go through the day and you see someone else doing something that gets you upset or something that offends you. Don't focus on the other person; focus on the action in and of itself, as part of a causal process, and then turn around and look at yourself. If, in your mind, you create other people out there, you create a lot of problems. But if you simply see life in the community as an opportunity to watch the principle of cause and effect as it plays itself out, the problems vanish.

The same with admirable people: You don't get jealous of their good qualities; you don't get depressed about the fact that you don't have their good qualities. Where do good qualities come from? They come from persistence, from effort, from training, which is something we can all do. So again, if you see something admirable in other people, *ask them about it*, and then try to apply those lessons in your own life. If we go through life without asking questions, we learn nothing. If we ask the wrong questions, we go off the path. If, with practice, we learn how to ask the right questions, that's the factor that helps us get our practice right on target.

I once read a man's reminiscences about his childhood in which he said that every day, when he'd come home from school, his mother's first question would be, "What questions did you ask in school today?" She didn't ask, "What did you learn? What did the teacher teach?" She asked, "What questions did you ask?" She was teaching him to think. So at the end of the day when you stop to reflect on the day's activities, that's a good question to ask yourself: "What questions did I ask today? What answers did I get?" That way you get to see which direction your practice is going.

Heightening the Mind

July, 2001

The Buddha concluded one of his most important talks with the phrase, *adhicitte ca ayogo,* commitment to the heightened mind. What this means is that we lift the mind above its ordinary concerns, as when we come here to practice meditation. Our normal cares of the day—looking after our own bodies, feeding them, looking after other people, being concerned with what other people think about us, how we interact with them, all the concerns of the day—we put those down, lift our mind above them, and bring it to the meditation object.

When you look at the affairs of the world, you see that they spin around just as the world does. There's a classic list of eight: gain and loss, status and loss of status, criticism and praise, pleasure and pain. These things keep trading places. You can't have the good ones without the bad ones. You can't have the bad ones without the good. They keep changing places like this, around and around, and if we allow our minds to get caught up in them it's like getting our clothes caught up in the gears of a machine. They keep pulling us in, pulling us in. If we don't know how to disentangle ourselves, they keep pulling us in until they mangle our arms, mangle our legs, crush us to bits. In other words, if we allow these preoccupations to consume the mind, the mind gets mangled and doesn't have a chance to be its own self.

We don't even know what the mind is like on its own because all we know is the mind as a slave to these things, running around wherever they force it. So when we come to meditate, we have to learn to lift our mind above these things. All thoughts of past and future we put aside. We just bring the mind to the breath so the mind doesn't have to spin around anymore. It simply stays with the breath coming in, going out, and gains at least some measure of freedom. From this heightened perspective we can look at our normal involvement with the world and begin to realize that, for the most part, it doesn't go anywhere. It just keeps spinning around, coming back to the same old places over and over and over again. All that gets accomplished is that the mind gets more and more worn out.

If we allow the mind to rise above these things so that it doesn't feed on them, doesn't run after them, we'll begin to get some sense of the mind's worth, in and of itself. As the mind gets still, things begin to settle out. Like sediment in a glass of water: If you allow the water to stay still for a time, whatever sediment is in there finally settles out and the water becomes clear.

This is what happens when you let the mind separate from its ordinary concerns and simply stay with its meditation. Even when you go back into your normal activities, you'll have a sense of the mind, your awareness, as something separate. This sense of "separate" is a very important part of the practice. It's part of the day-to-day work of practicing the Dhamma.

We all come to the practice hoping that some day some really great experiences are going to hit us while we're meditating. Well, they're not going to hit unless you do the day-to-day practice. This is why the Buddha insisted that there are four noble truths, not just the truth of the cessation of suffering, but also the tasks of understanding suffering, abandoning its cause, and developing the path. These are all very important parts of the teaching. They're all noble truths.

The development of the path is largely two things. One, developing qualities that enhance the mind's ability to know, to be aware. And then, two, learning how to let go of things that are burdensome to the mind. This is what it means to heighten the mind. Once you let go of the burdens, the mind gets lighter and begins to rise above things. Learning how to do this in all activities is very important because when the really Technicolor experiences hit in the meditation, if you can't rise above them you're just going to fall for them, too. And they eventually lead you back into the world again. Your attachments lead you back.

So a large part of the practice is learning how to lift your mind, stage by stage. You lift it above your ordinary, everyday activities and you get into a good state of concentration. In the beginning, the mind and the object seem to become one when you're really absorbed. But as you allow the mind to stay in that state for a while, it begins to separate out as well. You begin to see the object as one thing, your awareness as something else, and although they're right next to each other they *are* separate things.

This is what enables the mind to gain insight both into the workings of the mind and into the workings of its objects. It also develops the habit of learning how to let go, stage by stage. You rise from one level of concentration to the next to the next. You pull back. The image in the texts is of a person sitting up looking at a person lying down, or a person standing looking at a person sitting. You pull back bit by bit by bit, stage by stage. No matter how good the stage, you begin to realize you've got to lift above it.

This is especially important when really strong experiences come in the meditation. You don't jump to any conclusions. Again, you lift the mind above them and watch. Hopefully by that time the habit has become built-in enough so that you realize you can't allow yourself to get attached to anything, even the really amazing experiences. Lift yourself up rung by rung by rung along the ladder. You go from one attachment to a higher one to a higher one. Finally, though, there comes a point where you have to let go and just watch what happens. Only when you've developed this habit of lifting the mind up can you get through some of these experiences that waylay everyone else along the meditation path.

We're not just here for the experiences. We're learning the basic skills we need so that no matter what experience comes to the mind, we don't fall for it. We don't latch onto it so that we don't become a slave to it—for the whole purpose of the practice is freedom and yet the habits of the mind tend toward self-enslavement. Even when great feelings of oneness or unity or unlimitedness come into the mind, you find on a very subtle level that the mind can become enslaved to them as well. And the question is how, instead of becoming enslaved or enthralled, you can learn even from that kind of experience.

Ultimately the mind has to become totally free, even from the state of oneness, even from the state of unlimitedness, because a lot of those experiences are just states of concentration. There's still a subtle level of attachment and conditioning going on. But if you develop the habit of learning how to let go and rise above things even while you live in the midst of them, then you've developed the proper habits, the skills you need that are going to protect you in all circumstances.

There's a fine passage in one of Ajaan Maha Boowa's talks where, at the time of Ajaan Mun's death, he sits and reflects. At first he feels lost. Here is the teacher he was able to depend on for so long, and now that teacher is gone. What is he going to do? After a while he begins to realize: "Well, what were the things he taught when he was alive? Take those as your teachers." And one constant theme was: Whatever arises in the mind, if you don't get caught up with it but just stay with that sense of knowing, with the knowing as separate from the event in the mind, then, no matter what, that experience will pose no dangers for you.

This skill of learning how to step back, step back, raise the mind above its experiences: This is what's truly distinctive about the Buddha's teachings. This is what's distinctive about his approach to the really spectacular, non-dual experiences in the mind. If you haven't learned how to develop that approach to ordinary experiences in the mind—looking for the *use* of the experiences rather than trying to feed on them—then the spectacular ones are going to eat you up whole. This is why the habits developed along the path are so important. This is why the path is one of the four noble truths, on a par with the others.

So keep this teaching in mind, this issue of the heightened mind. Watch out for when you allow the mind to lie beneath its objects, under the power of its objects, and when you're able to lift it up above them, so that even though you live with them you have a sense of rising above them, of being able to use them, of not being caught up in them. That's the skill we're working on.

Respect for Concentration

July, 2001

We just chanted about having respect for concentration. This is an important principle to keep in mind because all too often the stillness of our minds is something we step on. An idea pops into our heads and we go running after it. We leave our home base very quickly and then find it hard to get back. We've got to learn how to make concentration our normal state of mind: centered, present, alert to the body, alert to things going on. It's not that you don't sense other things when you're concentrated, or that you don't register them with your senses at all. Simply that the mind doesn't move out after them. The mind stays firmly based in the breath, its home base, and from there it protects that sense of being centered, looks after it, maintains it. This is the only way that concentration can grow, can develop the real stability we need to withstand whatever comes up.

Too many times I've heard people say, "Now that my mind is calm, what do I do next?" They're in a great hurry to jump to the next step, to run off into insight. But before the mind can gain any liberating insight, it has to overcome its impatience to move. You need to get it very solid, very secure, because when you start working on the issues of insight—trying to understand why greed, anger, and delusion take over the mind—you're going to find yourself running up against all kinds of storms. If your concentration isn't really solid and settled, you'll just get blown away.

So you have to respect this part of the path. After all, it's the heart of the path. The Buddha once said that right concentration forms the heart of the noble eightfold path, while all the other factors of the path are simply requisites, supports for the right concentration, to keep it right, to keep it on track.

So have some respect for this quality of mind. Look after it. Sometimes it seems like we're going against the Buddha's teachings on inconstancy, stress, and not self when we focus on putting the mind in a state that's constant, easeful, and ours. We get really absorbed in this sense of oneness and we come to identify with it, both with the stillness and with the object of the stillness as well. It all becomes one. So it seems like we're running counter to what insight is supposed to tell us. But what we're actually doing is testing the limits of human effort. We're taking the *khandhas*—these aggregates of body, feeling, perception, thought-fabrications, and conscious-ness—and instead of identifying with them, we use them as tools. And as part of the process of mastering them as tools, there will have to be a sense of identification. You identify with the state of concen-tration, whatever sense of the body is present in the concentration, whatever feelings, perceptions, thought-fabrications, and conscious-ness are there. That's why you become so devoted to them. They all turn into a oneness. But instead of simply identifying with them, you're also treating them as the path. That makes all the difference.

You bring things together and, once they're brought together, you can sort them out for what they are. If everything is scattered all over the place it's hard to see how things interact, it's hard to see where the connections are, and where the lines are drawn between them. But when you get them all right here, gathered into one, then once they've been staying together for long while they begin to separate out.

Ajaan Lee has a nice image of taking a rock and putting it in a fire. When the various elements in the rock reach their melting point, they melt out of the rock, one at a time. That's how they separate. The same holds true with all the things you're going to try to understand and gain insight into. Once they've been together a long period of time, gathered here in a sense of oneness, they begin to separate out. And all you have to do is ask the question, "What's this? Is this the same as that?" And then you just watch. You begin to see that there's a natural dividing line between these things. But until you've brought the mind to oneness in concentration, you can't really see that. All the dividing lines you see are the ones imposed by words and ideas, by preconceived notions.

Put those preconceived notions aside and just focus on getting the mind centered. You're sitting here in concentration, trying to get the concentration as refined and as solid as possible. When you get up to leave, don't drop it. Try to maintain it. An image they use in the Canon is of a person carrying a bowl on his head, filled to the brim with oil. Try to develop that same sense of balance, care, and mindfulness. As you get up from concentration and go to wherever you're spending the night, try to maintain that sense of being centered and poised. Don't let it spill. This is one aspect of having respect for concentration: trying to maintain it throughout the course of the day, not letting yourself get distracted outside. Again, you'll be aware of outside things: people to talk to, work to be done, the sounds of the birds, the wind in the trees. These things will all be present to your awareness, but you won't send your attention out after them. Try to keep your center here inside.

As you develop this continuity, it becomes your habitual center of awareness, your habitual point of reference. The movement of other things in relation to that center becomes very clear. In other words, the impulse to go out and see something: You'll see it exactly as that—a current or a physical sensation in certain parts of the body that runs or flows out after things. If you can catch sight of it, you'll see: "Oh, that's what happens when the mind focuses its attention outside." There's both a mental and a physical side to that change of reference. When your sense of clear awareness is still enough, you can see these things as they move. The more still your frame of reference, the more refined the movements you can notice in the mind. So this element of stillness is very important. Without it, insight is just words, ideas, things you picked up from books. But with it, insight is seeing things as they actually happen, as they actually move.

So this is the basis from which insight comes, the insight that leads to release. You begin to observe the movements you used to ride on, because now you're not riding on them any more. You see these movements of the mind as they flash out, but you don't go flashing with them. That's what makes all the difference. If you ride out with them, that's just the way of the normal mind. But if there's a sense of being centered inside, you can see the movements of the mind as they go out, as thoughts go out, as perceptions go out, latching onto things. You see them as they actually happen. You begin to wonder, "Why would I ever want to identify with that?"

That's when the possibility of release comes. But this can happen only when you're really, really still. And to be still you'll need a sense of wellbeing here in the present moment. Otherwise, the mind won't stay. For the concentration to stay solid and unforced, you want to feel good being right here. You work with the breath in whatever way will help you to settle down, to stay clear and centered. As you use the breath to work through pain in the body, you'll find that some pains you can deal with and some pains you can't, but the only way you'll know is by experimenting. If there are pains you can't disperse by adjusting the breath, you learn to live with them. You learn not to identify with them. You're aware of them, but there's a sense of separation between the sense of awareness and the pain. That makes it bearable.

If you're going to identify with certain parts of the body, identify with the good ones. Find the parts of the body where you can maintain a sense of wellbeing through the breathing. Focus on those. Those become your center, your point of reference in the midst of this moving world.

The Uses of Pleasure & Pain

August, 2001

Allow your awareness to settle in on the breath and get aligned with the body. It takes a little experimenting to find exactly what amount of pressure is needed, what amount of force is needed to stay with the breath and the body in a way that's just right. If the pressure is too light, the mind goes drifting off. If it's too heavy, the body starts feeling constricted, the mind starts feeling constricted, and it's going to look for a way to get out.

So try to see precisely what amount of mindfulness and alertness is needed just to keep the body and mind together right at the breath. The breath will be a good barometer to let you know when the pressure is too much, when it's too little—but you've got to know how to read the barometer.

This is why we practice meditation day after day after day, to get more familiar with our barometer. To begin with, you can focus your awareness at any one spot in the body where the sensation of breathing is very clear. It might be the tip of the nose, the throat, the middle of the chest, the abdomen, any spot where you know clearly: "Now the breath is coming in, now the breath is going out." There's a sense of rightness about the spot; it's an easy spot to maintain your focus.

This may seem strange, this emphasis on ease and comfort in the meditation after everything we've heard about the Buddha's teachings on pain, stress, and suffering. But you have to look carefully at what he says about pain, stress, and suffering and also what he has to say about pleasure. Look at the four noble truths. Truth number one, of course, is stress and suffering. But buried down in number four, the path, you find the most important factor of the path, right concentration, which involves getting the mind focused on the breath with a sense of ease and rapture. This rapture comes from seclusion: seclusion here meaning that you're not thinking about past, not thinking about the future, you're right here with the present moment. Things are settling in, and there's a snugness to how things feel. It feels good, it feels secure, being right here.

Look at what the Buddha has to say about the tasks with regard to each of the noble truths. The task with regard to stress and suffering is to comprehend it. The task with regard to the path is to develop it, which means you want to develop that sense of ease, the sense of rapture that comes as the mind begins to settle down in concentration. What you're doing is taking one of the aggregates—the aggregate of feeling—and instead of latching onto it or pushing it away, you learn how to use it as a tool.

When pain and stress and suffering come, you want to comprehend them. Comprehending pain and stress teaches you a lot about the mind. The Buddha never said that life is suffering. He just said there's suffering *in* life, which is a very different teaching. As long as there's going to be pain, as long as there's going to be suffering, get the most use out of them. You find as you focus on pain—as you get to know it, get to comprehend it—that you learn all kinds of things about how the mind is working. In particular, you learn to see what it's doing to take a physical pain and turn it into mental pain—or, if you're starting with mental pain, to make it worse.

But to watch that feeling of pain long enough and consistently enough so that you can comprehend it, the mind needs strength, it needs nourishment. Otherwise it gets drained. That's where the pleasure in the path comes in. That's your nourishment. Try to create a sense of wellbeing in the mind as it's focused in the present moment so that it doesn't feel threatened by the pain, doesn't feel drained by the pain, so that you always have a place to go when you need that strength.

What we're doing is taking one of the aggregates that we usually cling to.... Clinging here doesn't mean just holding on. It also means trying to push away, and pushing away is like pushing away a glob of tar. The more you push it away, the more you get stuck. So instead of clinging or pushing away, we try to learn how to use these aggregates as tools, in the same way you'd use tar to make asphalt for paving a road.

This is a common theme running throughout the Buddha's teachings: Before you can let go of anything, you have to learn how to master it. Otherwise, you're just holding on, pushing away, holding on, pushing away. And nothing comes from that except more stress, more suffering, more pain. This harms not only you but also the people around you. If you're constantly feeling worn down by the pains and the inconveniences of life, you'll find it hard to be kind to other people. In fact, most of the evil things people do in their lives come from their sense of being totally overwhelmed, feeling weak and trapped and then lashing out.

But if you give the mind the sense of strength and security that comes with knowing it has a center it can return to and gain nourishment from, it's a gift not only to yourself but also to the people around you. It's not a selfish practice.

Learn how not to hold onto feelings, grabbing hold of the pleasant ones, pushing the painful ones away. Instead, learn how to use them as tools. When they're used as tools, they open things up in the mind. You understand where the mind is unskillful in how it manages its thinking, and you realize that you don't have to be unskillful. There are better ways to think, better ways to manage the thought processes in the mind.

And a funny thing happens. As you master these processes, they bring you to a point where everything reaches equilibrium. That's where you can really let go. You can even let go of your tools at that point because they've taken you where you want to go. From that point on, everything opens up to the Deathless.

But you can't get there by pushing and pulling your way around. If the Deathless were something you could force your way into, everybody would have gone to nibbana a long time ago. It requires a lot of finesse, a lot of skill in how you deal with the mind, learning to recognize the time for analyzing issues of stress and suffering, and the time for letting the mind rest so it that it can gain strength and then go back to work.

The ultimate skill is learning how to put those two things together. In other words, you develop states of concentration to give the mind a really solid center, and from that center you can begin to let go of things that are obviously unskillful, things you obviously don't want to hang on to. Then when you've let go of everything else, you turn on that pleasant center you've been developing and take it apart. But all too often we've read the books that tell us what comes next in the practice and we want to get on to insight as fast as possible. In doing so, we tend to destroy the very quality that's going to help us: this ability to get the mind aligned with the body in a way that feels just right and then to use the strength, use the nourishment the comes from that, the stillness and ease, the steadiness that comes from that. Only then can you really gain insight.

In other words, you just can't jump over concentration or go rushing through the various levels. It's something you want to settle down into, so that you can stay still, calm, for long periods of time. And when you can stay that way during your formal sitting, you take it out and try to maintain that same calm center no matter where you go, no matter what happens. That's when you really gain interesting insights into the mind, seeing how it goes flowing out after things, rushing to grab hold of this, rushing to push that away.

The Buddha talks about effluents in the mind, things flowing out of the mind, and when you can maintain your center you actually get a physical sense of the energy flowing out as the mind loses its alignment with the body and goes out after its objects. The trick is learning how to maintain that still, steady observer so that you can see the movement and realize you don't have to go along with it. The movement is something separate. The knower is something separate. And the movement dies away.

When you have that separation clearly delineated, you can see even more clearly which of the mind's actions are skillful and which are not. You begin to see cause and effect in a way that really opens things up in the mind.

So we carry these five *khandhas,* these aggregates, around with us, and the wisdom of the Buddha is in taking these aggregates that tend to weigh us down, like big lumps of metal in a suitcase, and opening up the suitcase to look inside. That's when you begin to see that they're not just lumps of metal. They're tools, tools that you can apply to dismantling your attachments so you don't have to lug things around any more. Use them to cut away your obvious attachments and then finally, when everything else is taken care of, you can let go of your attachments to the tools themselves. But until that point, you want to take good care of them—not to the point of worshipping them, but careful enough that they stay in good shape so you can actually use them.

This is why the Buddha didn't teach self-torment, but he didn't teach self-indulgence, either. The middle path between the two is not half indulgence and half torment. It's learning how to regard these aggregates as tools. You've got aggregates of form, feeling, perception, thought-fabrications, and consciousness. Learn how to treat them as tools, showing them the proper care and attention that tools need, but also realizing that they're not the be-all and end-all of life. They're processes, not things. They've got their uses, but they're not ends in and of themselves.

Once you've got that point clear, the path opens up.

An Introduction to Pain

March, 2002

So many people accuse the Buddha of being pessimistic: He starts his teachings with pain. And yet when you first sit and meditate, what do you find after the first five or ten minutes? Pain. You can't avoid it. Or when people just can't sit by themselves, can't spend a whole day by themselves without busying themselves with this, that, or the other thing, what's the problem? It's mental pain, mental discomfort. These are things we live with all the time, and yet we think somehow that if people point them out, they're being pessimistic. Of course, the Buddha's purpose in pointing out pain and suffering wasn't just to stop right there, pointing them out and saying, "Isn't that horrible." He says, "Look. There's a solution." In fact, his approach to pain is extremely optimistic: Human beings can put an end to suffering, in this lifetime, through their own efforts.

So when we sit here, we have to anticipate that there will be pain in sitting still. The reason we normally move around is because we encounter pain in a particular posture, so we change a little bit to get away from it. The Buddha's approach isn't to try to run away from it that way. He says, "Look into it."

As Ajaan Suwat used to say, "We normally take our cravings as our friends and our pains as our enemies. We should switch that around. Learn to look at pain as your friend, and craving as your enemy." The craving is what's really causing all the problems. The pain is just there to teach you something. Of course, it's a difficult friend. Some people are easy to be friends with; you can get along with them with no problem at all. Others are difficult. Pain is definitely a difficult friend, but one worth cultivating. Still, because it's difficult, you have to go about it the right way.

This is why, when we start meditating, the Buddha doesn't have us focus immediately on the pain. He says to focus on the breath instead, because whatever pain is associated with the breath—and it tends to be subtle, but it *is* there—is something you can manage, something you can deal with. He gives you the breath as your tool for dealing with the pain. So when you're aware of pain, don't yet let your primary focus be on the pain. Keep your focus on the breath. In other words, get used to being acquainted with the breath first, because that's the person who'll introduce you to pain properly. It's like meeting any important person: You first have to get to know certain well-connected friends who can introduce you to that person. And that's the way it is with pain: You have to know the breath first, for it's your well-connected friend.

So get in touch with the breath. Find a place in the body that's relatively at ease, relatively comfortable, and focus there first; get to know that spot first; be very sensitive to the breathing at that spot. When you breathe in there, how does it feel? When you breathe out there, how does it feel? Is there even the slightest discomfort? Can you make it feel better? Can you experiment with different ways of breathing, different ways of conceiving the breath energy in your body? When you find something that feels really good, the whole tone of your body will feel really good. Instead of sitting here tensely trying to breathe in one spot, think of the whole body relaxing into the breath. The more relaxed you are about the practice, the longer you'll be able to stay with it. So think of yourself as just relaxing into the body, relaxing into the breath. Find a way of breathing that feels really good—all the way from the beginning to the end as it goes in, and all the way from the beginning to the end as it goes out. Make that your foundation.

Once that feels good, think of spreading that good breath energy to the other parts of the body. Think of it as going right through the pain. Many times a lot of the discomfort we feel around pain comes from tensing up around it, and the tensing-up just makes things worse. So try to breathe through any tension you feel. Breathe right through the pain, all the way on out. Suppose there's a pain in your hip or in your knee: Think of the breath going through the hip, through the knee, all the way out through the toes as you breathe in, and out into the air as you breathe out. As you approach the pain, try to maintain the same mental tone and feeling tone you had when focusing on the comfortable breath. Your primary frame of reference here should still be the breath. There's no way you're *not* going to notice the pain, but ask yourself, "How does the breath affect the pain? How does the pain affect the breath?" Always keep the breath in mind as your frame of reference. That gives you a handle on the pain. Otherwise if you jump right into the pain, you find yourself picking up the energy from the pain that puts you on edge. The first thing you'll think will be: "Make the pain go away." And then there's even more impatience as you get involved in the past and the future of the pain.

But when you stay with the breath, you want to be as much with the present as possible. Don't think about how long the pain has been there or how long it's going to stay. Just, "What's there right now?" That takes one *huge* burden off the mind right there. So as you go through the pain, make the thread of your awareness stay with the breath. That's what you want to keep track of; that's what you want to hold onto. Learn to relate to the pain through the breath rather than just butting up against the pain head-on.

Now, if you find that the pain just gets worse and worse and worse to the point where you can't stand it, sit with it another five minutes and then change your position. In other words, push your limits a bit at a time and you'll find that you get better and better at staying with the pain, more skillful in maintaining your frame of reference with the breath. As long as you really stay with the breath you'll be okay. Slipping away from the breath is what creates the problems, because the mind then immediately creates stories about the pain, creates issues around the pain: "Why is this pain happening to me?" Or if it's a physical pain that you know you caused: "Why did I do that?" All these questions—"How much longer is it going to last? Am I going to have this pain the rest of my life?"— just drop them right now. Stay with the breath. Deal immediately in the present, because the past and the future are not actually there. They are things the mind creates, and once they're created they turn around and bite the mind. So try to stay with that thread of the breath as it goes through the pain.

Then you'll begin to see why the Buddha focused on pain as *the primary spiritual issue* in our practice, for it teaches you so much about the mind. It's like filming a documentary on the animals in the desert: If you go out and spend the day wandering around the desert, you'll probably miss most of the animals. But if you set up your camera at a safe place near the water hole 24 hours a day, all of the animals in the area are going to have to come there. That's where you get to film them all. It's the same with the pain. If you focus steadily on the pain, you'll see all the mind's reactions around the pain. All its issues will come to the surface and congregate there.

At the same time, if you use the breath as your tool for dealing with the pain, those issues won't totally overwhelm you. It's like having a safe shelter to run to if the lions object to being filmed. You've got a safe place in the breath. You're not totally at the mercy of the pain. You can pull out any time you want, and you've got a handle to deal with it. You've established a feeling tone around the whole body that holds the pain, not grasping onto it, but surrounding it with an energy, surrounding it with a space where you're not threatened by it. *Then* you can deal with it. When you're not threatened, you can really get into the present moment. If you find that you can't yet handle it, you've got the breath to go back to.

But when things get stable enough in the mind, clear enough in the mind so that you can handle it, then you really can start looking at the pain as your friend. You can get familiar enough with it so that ultimately you can understand it for what it truly is, so that ultimately it's no longer a problem. Until that point, it's always going to be a difficult friend, but if you start off on the right foot, using the breath as the basis of your friendship, you'll find that you're in a good position to make the friendship work.

A Dependable Mind

November 10, 1996

Our basic problem in life is that the most important thing in our lives is the thing we know the least about: our own minds. As the Buddha said, all things come out of the mind—all our experiences, all the happiness and all the pain we experience, come from the mind. "All things have the mind as their forerunner. Things are made of the mind, determined by the mind"—and yet we don't know our minds, so our lives are out of control. We don't understand where things come from or how things happen in our lives. That's why we have to meditate—to get to know our own minds.

The difficulty in meditation is that you can't focus directly on the mind. It's like focusing on the wind up in a sky with no clouds—you have no way of knowing which direction it's going because there's nothing against which it's going to make contact. That's why you need a meditation object like the breath or *"buddho"* or parts of the body. Whichever object you find easy to settle down with, that's the one you take. Having an object gives the mind something to bounce off of—because when you decide you're going to stay with something, you begin to see how erratic the mind is. It keeps jumping around. It goes here a little while, then it goes there for a little while, and then over there. You begin to realize how this most important element in life—the mind—is so totally out of control, totally undependable. That's why the mind needs training. We need to strap it down to one object and make it stay there so that we can really get to know it and train it until we sense that we can depend on it.

We talk about taking refuge in the Buddha, the Dhamma, and the Sangha, but they can be our refuge only when we bring them into the mind. And the mind can be dependable only when we've got the qualities of the Buddha, Dhamma, and Sangha in there: qualities like mindfulness, concentration, persistence, and dependability. So if you want to depend on the mind, make it something you *can* depend on.

The Buddha's good news is that it's possible to do this. At the time the Buddha was teaching, there were other teachers who said that there is nothing that you can do about the way life is, it's all written in the stars. Others said that no matter what we do, any action leads to more suffering, so the only way to stop suffering is to stop acting. And still others said that life is totally chaotic, there's no way you can make any sense out of it at all, so don't try. Just try to have as much fun as you can while you can because everything falls apart at death. So there were all kinds of teachings, but they were all teachings lacking in hope. The Buddha's teaching was the only one that offered any hope. He said, yes, there is a skill that you can develop in training the mind and, yes, it does lead to true happiness.

So just as with developing any skill, you have to be observant, stick with it, be sensitive to what you're doing, be sensitive to the results, make necessary changes or adjustments and, as a result, you keep getting better and better and better at it. Sometimes the improvement is hard to see because it's so incremental. It takes such tiny, tiny steps, but you can rest assured that whatever positive energy you put into the practice is going to produce positive results. That's also part of the good news of the Buddha's teachings. Nothing good you do is wasted. No effort that you put into Right Effort is wasted.

So we have conviction in the Buddha's teaching because he teaches us to have conviction in ourselves—that the practice is something we *can* do. We don't have to depend on anything from the outside at all. Your own power, your own potential: That's what's going to get you where you want to go. If you have to depend on others, you don't really know if you can depend on them or not. Will they be there when you need them? They might change their minds. After all, you have no control over things outside of you.

Even though you currently may not have much control over the mind, you can still work at it and develop more and more control over time. Tell the mind to sit down and stay in one place often enough, and eventually it will stay. It's going to rebel for a while, but if you use your ingenuity in teaching it—showing it that in being obedient this way it won't always have to be struggling or suffering—it's going to find that it actually likes settling down. And then you can hardly keep it from settling down—it wants to keep coming back, coming back, coming back to the state of stillness, feeling at home in the present moment.

This is why we adjust the breath in the practice: to help the mind settle down easily. And we work to get to know the breath. What are the different ways it has of coming in? What are the different ways it has of going out? How does it affect the rest of the body?

When the breath comes in and out, it's not just the air coming in and out of the lungs. It's the energy that courses through the whole body, throughout every nerve. Think about the whole nervous system going down from the brain, down the backbone, out the arms, out the legs, encompassing all the parts of the body. Then allow yourself to think that the entire system can be affected by the breath if you let it happen. Let the whole body relax and get into the breathing. Let your mind get into the breathing. Don't think of yourself as being outside someplace looking at the breath. Be immersed in the process of breathing. The whole body breathes in. The whole body breathes out. And you're right in there with it.

After you work at this for a while, you begin to find that the work pays off. It really feels good, feels gratifying, just to sit here breathing. The mind has a sense of being at home. If the mind were to go out to think of other things, you'd be sending it out into a territory it totally has to create for itself. But you don't have to create much right here in the present moment. When you're really with the breath, you're putting much less of a strain on the mind. And when the mind gets used to this, it decides that it really likes it. Until it decides that it likes it, you have to use both the carrot and the stick. The carrot is the comfortable sensation of breathing; the stick is the constant reminder of what's going to happen if the mind doesn't come under control, if it isn't willing to settle down—all the suffering and pain that you'll have to endure.

The Buddha said that when people suffer, when there's pain in life, they have two kinds of reactions. One is bewilderment because they don't know where the pain comes from or why it's happening. The second reaction is the desire to get free of the pain one way or another. And these two reactions go hand in hand. You're bewildered at the same time that you're trying to get free, and so you tend to do all kinds of unskillful things to get away from the pain, things that aren't helpful at all. But through practice you come to realize that the pain in the body isn't the culprit. The pain in the mind—the mental anguish, the mental distress: That's the real problem. When you really get to know the mind you see that the pain in the body isn't such a big deal at all. It becomes a problem only when the mind takes it on and converts it into mental pain, but to understand mental pain you have to work with physical pain.

So after the mind has settled down, focus it on the pain: pain in the legs, pain in the back, whatever. Just get to know it as it's actually present. What is this pain? Is it what you think it is? Try to see the pain on its own—simply as a sensation, and not as a "pain"—without all the presuppositions you may have about it: that it's placed right here, that it has this shape, that it's taken over the body, or whatever crazy notion the mind has about the pain.

When you think about it, most of the notions you've developed about pain were developed when you were really small, because that's when you first met up with pain. The first thing they do when you're born is to spank you so you can breathe. And even before they spank you, going through the process of birth is enough to make you pass out. So we've been dealing with pain ever since we were small, and for most of us the strategies we've been using are those we picked up when we were so small that we didn't know what was going on. A lot of those strategies are still there in your mind.

So just sit down and get to know the pain. Simply regarding the pain as something you want to know changes a lot of your subconscious attitudes toward it right there. Your usual attitude is that once there's pain, you want to get rid of it, to get away from it. Of course, if you keep running away from it you're never going to get to know it, you'll never get to understand it, and this means that you'll end up dealing with pain more and more out of bewilderment. So once the mind has settled down in the sense of wellbeing fostered by the breath, tell yourself that it's time to get to know the pain, make friends with the pain—not so you can live with pain forever, but so you can really understand how far the pain goes, how far the mind goes, and where the two are actually separate. Be sure that your purpose is to get to know the pain, not so much to make it go away, but to thoroughly understand it. The understanding is what will enable you to get beyond it in ways you didn't expect: The mind can be with the pain and yet not be pained by it.

This is an important skill to develop because as long as there's a body, there's going to be pain. The question is not how to run away from it, but how to live with it so as not to be pained by it. Realize that the pain is simply happening, not necessarily happening to *you*. It's just happening. It's an event. It has no intention to harm you at all. You feel pained by it because you put yourself in the way by laying claim to the part of the body where the pain seems to be. It's like getting into the line of fire: You're bound to get shot. So don't get into the line of fire. Don't lay any claim to it. See that the pain is just something that's there, and that it's going to come and it's going to go in line with its own causes and effects.

Your only duty is to watch it, to see what it's really like for there to be pain. Simply be there with the pure sensation in the moment. How does it move around? How does it change? Exactly what about it is painful? What's the mind doing to the pain when the mind labels it? What effect does that have? If you can catch that event in the mind—the mind saying, "This is this and that is that; this is the pain and it's doing this," and all of the other running commentary that the mind makes on the present moment—then you begin to realize this in itself is a lot of the problem right there. The fear that the pain is going to stay; the anticipation that it's going to stay; all these thoughts: Just let them drop away. See what happens. Where does the pain go when they drop away? By watching this your whole attitude toward the pain changes, because you come to see that it isn't at all what you thought it was.

And at the same time you learn an awful lot about your mind—all the things that the mind comes in and says about the pain. It's as if you have a whole committee offering their suggestions and opinions. So this is a very good way of getting to know the mind because a lot of things buried in the mind will tend to surface and focus on what's happening when there's pain. Instead of trying to run away from the pain, you just sit with it and see what kind of reaction comes up in the mind. Again, don't identify with the reactions. The reactions will say, "Stop, stop, stop." Or they'll say, "This is this and that's that and you should do this and you should do that." Just respond, "No, I'm just going to be here. I'm just going to watch." And watch both the pain and the mind's reactions to the pain.

This is how you really get to know the mind while training it to become more and more dependable. If the mind isn't shaken by pain, there's very little that's going to shake it. If it doesn't fear pain, there's very little for it to fear. And when it's not afraid in the face of pain, it becomes a mind you can depend on. When you want it to work, it will work for you. When you want it to rest, it will rest. When you want it to think, it can think—and it will think clearly. When the time comes for it to stop thinking, it will stop.

We've spent so much of our lives developing fear of pain, fear of suffering. If you can get past that fear, get past the mind's tendency to be pushed around by these things, you've got a mind you can rely on. As when they train soldiers: They have to put the soldiers through all kinds of hell in order to know which ones they can depend on and which ones they can't. The ones who come through it okay: Those are the ones you know you can depend on. It's the same with the mind. If you're afraid to face up to pain, the mind will never have any control over itself at all. It will never become something you really can depend on. It will always flinch under the pain, unwilling to do this, unwilling to do that, because it's afraid. And when that's what your mind is like, where are you going to find anything to depend on? Where are your true friends at that point? Even your own mind isn't a friend.

So when the mind has settled down and really feels at home in the present moment, working with pain is an excellent way of training it. Through this you can come to see that the mind will obey you not only when you make it comfortable, but also when you test it, when you give it work to do. That's when you have a mind you can really take as your refuge.

The Components of Suffering

May, 2003

Let your mind settle in. Stay with the breath. There's nowhere else you have to go, nothing else you have to do right now. Just be with your breathing. When the breath comes in, you know it's coming in. When the breath goes out, you know it's going out. Allow it to come in and go out in a way that feels good and refreshing. If you're feeling tired, you may want to breathe in a way that's energizing. If you're feeling frenetic, breathe in a way that's more calming. Gain a sense of what the breath can do for the body and the mind here in the present moment.

Do what you can to put the mind in a good mood. In other words, if you approach the process of meditation with a lot of anxiety, with a lot of frustration, that anxiety and frustration will show up in the breath and simply make things worse. So remind yourself: Not too much is demanded of you right now, just being with the breath. If you notice you've wandered off, just bring the mind right back. If it wanders off again, bring it back again and try to make the breath even more comfortable. As you keep at this, you find that the mind develops a stronger and stronger foundation, a place where it can stay, a place where it really feels safe, where it feels at home, where it can look at the larger issues in life and not mess them up.

The Buddha talks about suffering as his number one truth, and when we hear about that, many of us want to run away. We feel that we have enough suffering in life; we don't want to hear about it anymore. But the Buddha's whole reason for teaching about suffering is because he has a cure. To work that cure, though, you first have to get the mind in good shape, because most of us, when we deal with suffering, simply make the issue worse. We feel threatened by it, we feel surrounded by it, we start getting desperate, and in our desperation we do all kinds of things that are harmful, both to ourselves and to people around us.

So first get the mind in a good mood. All you need is the breath coming in and out with a sense of wellbeing. If you're really observant and become familiar with the breath over time, you find that that sense of wellbeing starts permeating throughout other parts of your life as well. And when you've got a sense of wellbeing you can depend on, *then* you can turn to the issue of suffering to see exactly what suffering is, looking at it not so much out of desperation as out of curiosity. As the Buddha said, the best way to deal with suffering is to comprehend it, as in the passage we chanted just now. He said most people don't discern suffering. We suffer, we feel it, but we don't discern it, we don't understand it. The Buddha said that if you understand it, you can manage it, you can put an end to it. If you don't understand it, you just keep on suffering and never put an end to it at all.

In his first sermon he describes suffering: the suffering of birth, the suffering of aging, the suffering of illness, the suffering of death, of being separated from what you love, of being conjoined with things you don't like, of not getting what you want. That seems to be a pretty good summation, but then he boils it down to even more basic terms. This is where the discussion gets technical. He analyses suffering down to five heaps, five clinging-aggregates: form imbued with clinging, feeling imbued with clinging, perceptions, thought-fabrications, and consciousness, all imbued with clinging. The clinging is the important element. It's what turns ordinary form, feeling, and so forth, into suffering.

We're often told that these aggregates are the Buddha's description of what we are, but that wasn't his purpose in formulating this teaching. His purpose was to give us tools for breaking suffering down into manageable pieces. For most of us, suffering is an enormous issue, much larger and more pressing than the abstract question of who or what we are. When suffering comes, it overwhelms us. We can't stand up under its weight. In fact that's one of the traditional definitions of suffering: that which is hard to bear.

And it's hard to bear because we feel overwhelmed. When it hits hard, it seems like an enormous mountain filling our awareness. We can't get a handle on it. The purpose of dividing it into these five heaps is to break the mountain down into gravel, and the gravel down into dust. This helps us realize that no matter what the type of suffering—whether it's the suffering of aging, illness, death, the suffering of separation, the suffering of not getting what we want—it can all be analyzed into just five sorts of things. That's all it is. And furthermore we can look at these five sorts of things and see that there's nothing there worth suffering over. We build enormous narratives around our pains, but what are those narratives? They're just perceptions combined with the thought-fabrications built out of them. If we cling to those narratives they're going to make us suffer. But if we take them apart, we see that there's nothing much there.

So the Buddha has us focus, not so much on the story line, but on the building blocks we use to put the story line together. If you get down to the building blocks, you begin to see how artificial this whole process is—because these aggregates are not things. They're actually activities, things we do. We suffer because we cling to certain activities, certain movements of the mind. So to cut through this clinging, you have to keep breaking your suffering down and analyzing it: What's going on here? Suppose there's a pain in your leg and you're suffering from it. What's going on there? There's the form of the body, and then there are the actual feelings of pain. And then there are the perceptions, the labels you put on the feeling; the thought-fabrications, the stories you build around the feeling; and then the consciousness, the repeated acts of being conscious of all these things.

So instead of building up the stories around the feeling—getting angry about the feeling, getting upset about it, worrying about it—if the mind is calm enough you can start taking the suffering surrounding the feeling apart. What's going on? What's actually there? There's the form of the body, which is actually separate from the feeling, although we often glom the two together. If there's a pain in our knee, it feels like our whole knee is nothing but pain. But if you look at it carefully, there's the form of your body, and then there are the feelings flickering around the form. They're not a single, solid thing. Many times we perceive the feeling to be a solid thing, but now we're taking that perception apart. Actually there's not just one perception. There are many repeated perceptions, just as there are many moments of feeling. This is why these things are called *khand-has,* or heaps. Like heaps of gravel or heaps of sand, they're made out of small individual events, small individual motions, either physical motions or mental motions. So you break them down, break them down. And once they're broken down, they're not too big to handle. You can change them. For example, those perceptions you applied to the feelings: What happens if you change them from perceptions of "pain" to simply perceptions of "sensation"?

Or you can try to analyze the sensation into its physical aspects: the sensation of warmth or heat, or maybe a sense of blockage that feels solid. If you actually take those solid feelings apart, though, you begin to see they're not so solid after all.

Then there are the stories you build up around the sensations, the fears of what will happen if you don't do something about the pain. If you sit here for the next hour, is your leg going to fall off? Will you harm the tissues of the body by cutting off the blood? The mind can build up all sorts of stories about the sensations, but instead of looking at the stories and getting caught up in the story line, just look at them as words coming through the mind without your having to believe them. Simply watch the stories as individual words. Then you begin to see that if you cling to the story line, you make the pain worse. So why cling to it? You don't have to follow the story line. It's not a movie you've paid to see. You're not missing anything important if you don't follow it through to the end.

So what you want to do is take the suffering apart into its component parts and locate the clinging that turns those component parts into the suffering. If you take each component part on it's own, it's not all that bad. The aggregate itself is not suffering. There can be a pain in the leg but we suffer simply because we identify with it, we lay claim to it as ours. That's why we suffer. Without the act of identification, without the clinging, there would be no suffering. The mental label that says "mine" or "my pain," "my leg," or whatever: What happens if you drop it? You don't have to think it. There's nobody forcing you to think it. There's simply the force of habit. And habits can be changed.

As you take the suffering apart into little bits and pieces like this, it's a lot more manageable. Many times the pain may still be there, but there's no suffering. Or sometimes when you're not worked up about it, the pain actually goes away. Some physical pains are physical in their causes; others are more mental in theirs. Even physical pain has its mental component, as the mind chooses which sensations to focus on and which ones to ignore, which ones to downplay and which ones to magnify with its stories and running commentary. You can see this mental component clearly when you stop the commentary, or when you just step back and watch the commentary as you would something curious, and say "Well, why would I believe that?", and suddenly the suffering goes away. Whether or not the pain is still there, the suffering is gone. That's when you see that the issue was not the pain but the unnecessary suffering you created by clinging to these feelings and perceptions. When you see clearly the things you've been clinging to, and that they're not really worth clinging to, the suffering breaks down. The mountain is leveled and pulverized into dust. When you've mastered this skill, that's the end of suffering.

Giving Rise to Discernment

October 29, 2002

We meditate, developing mindfulness, developing concentration, and after a while we begin to wonder, "When is the discernment going to come? When are the insights going to come?" So it's instructive to look at the Buddha's analysis of what gives rise to discernment. Mindfulness and concentration are prerequisites, but there's more. And in searching for that "more," it's especially instructive to look at two sets of qualities that the Buddha said lead to Awakening—the five strengths and the seven factors for Awakening—to learn their lessons on what gives rise to discernment, what's needed for insights to arise. Otherwise you can meditate for twenty, thirty, forty years—as Ajaan Lee says, you could die and your body could dry out on the spot—and still not gain any discernment, because you're lacking some of the proper qualities.

The five strengths—a set of factors that culminate in discernment—are interesting because they start out, not with ideas that you've heard from someone else in terms of what Buddhist discernment is about. They start with the quality of conviction. Conviction in what? Conviction in the principle of kamma. That's what it comes down to—conviction in the principle that our actions do matter. Some people have problems with the teaching on kamma, but what exactly is the Buddha asking you to believe in when he asks you to have conviction in kamma? First, action really is happening—it's not an illusion. Second, you really are responsible for your actions. There's no outside force like the stars or some good or evil being acting through you. When you're conscious, you're the one who decides what to do. Third, your actions have results—you're not just writing on the water—and those results can be good or bad depending on the quality of the intention behind the act.

So the teaching on kamma puts you in charge of shaping your life. It's a good teaching to believe in. And how does this relate to discernment? It provides the basis for the questions you're going to ask to give rise to discernment. And because the principle of kamma places a lot of emphasis on the need to act on skillful intentions to get the good results you want, the basic question becomes: How can you tell whether an intention is skillful or unskillful?

Together with conviction you need the quality of heedfulness: the realization that if you're not careful about your actions you can create a lot of suffering for yourself and for those around you. Heedfulness is said to underlie the development of the five strengths leading up to discernment. It's the quality that makes sure you're going to pay close attention to what you're doing, close attention to your intentions, close attention to the results of your actions—as in the passage where the Buddha's instructing Rahula, his son. Before you do something, he tells Rahula, ask yourself, "What's the intention here? Why am I doing this? Is it going to lead to suffering or not?" Only if the intention looks good should you act on it. Then, while you're acting, you check the results of your action. After the action is done you check again, because while some results are immediate, others are long term. So conviction in kamma focuses your attention at the right spot and gets you asking the right questions. Heedfulness gives urgency to your investigation. And the two of them together lead to discernment.

The teachings on the seven factors for Awakening are similar. You start out with mindfulness. The Buddha teaches you to be mindful of the body in and of itself, feelings in and of themselves, mind states, mental qualities in and of themselves. Why? So that you can be really clear on what your actions are and what the results are. If you're concerned with other issues—as the Buddha says, "things in the world," things that other people are doing— you miss what *you're* doing. So you focus right here, get yourself in the present moment, not simply because the present moment is a good moment in and of itself, but because it's the only place where you're going to see your intentions in action.

In this way, mindfulness puts you in a position to develop the second factor for Awakening: the discernment factor, called "analysis of qualities." The qualities here are qualities in the mind, mental states, in the present. The food for this factor is appropriate attention to the skillful and unskillful states arising in the mind. You pay attention to the intentions you act on, trying to see what's skillful and what's not. And again the test for judging whether your actions are skillful is by their results: How much harm do they cause? How much happiness? Discernment focuses on actions in terms of cause and effect, and works at developing greater and greater skill in acting, greater and greater sensitivity in evaluating and learning from the results of your actions, to the point where your actions are so skillful that they lead to the Deathless.

This may sound unusual, for we're often taught that Buddhist discernment focuses on seeing things in terms of the three characteristics: inconstancy, stress, and not-self. We're taught to look for the inconstancy, the impermanence of things, and then to see that if they're inconstant they must be stressful; if they're stressful they must be not-self. Well, those teachings have to be placed in context, and that context is the act of judging the results of our actions. The three characteristics are designed so that we don't content ourselves with only a middling level of skillfulness. In other words, you might be skillful enough to have a good job, a nice place to live, a good family life—in other words, ordinary, mundane wellbeing—and a lot of people get satisfied right there. Or you might get satisfied with a nice state of concentration. You might be able to get the mind centered pretty much at will; things don't disturb you too much. A lot of people stop right there—it's good enough for them.

This is where the teachings on the three characteristics kick in, in judging the results of your actions: "Are they really satisfactory? Do they give permanent, constantly dependable results?" Well, no. If they don't, then you're setting yourself up for stress, suffering, disappointment. You're setting yourself to latch onto things that aren't totally under your control. In other words, they're not yours. You can't say, "Okay, body, don't get old. Go back and get younger, the way you were, say, five or ten years ago." You can't tell your painful feelings to turn into pleasure. You can't arrange for only good and useful thoughts to come into your mind. The purpose of the three characteristics is to keep you from getting complacent. They help foster heedfulness, so that your standards for judging your actions stay high. In judging the results of your actions, you're not going to settle for anything that falls under the three characteristics. You'll keeping trying to become more skillful in your actions until you gain results that aren't inconstant or stressful, results where self and not-self don't apply.

In modern culture it's considered psychologically unhealthy to set very high standards for yourself. What does that do? It creates a society of very middling people, mediocre people, people who experience a mediocre level of happiness. The Buddha, though, was very demanding, first with himself, and then with his followers. He said, "Don't satisfy yourself with just ordinary, everyday wellbeing," because it's not well all the time. When you set your sights, set them on something of more permanent value, what he called "the noble search": the search for what doesn't age, doesn't grow ill, doesn't die, for a happiness that doesn't change.

So the three characteristics in and of themselves are not the totality of Buddhist wisdom, Buddhist discernment. They have to be placed in context, the context of the question of skillfulness: "What are you doing? What are your intentions? What are the results of your actions based on those intentions? Are you content with them or do you want better?" The three characteristics spur you on to be more demanding of yourself, saying, "I want better than this. I've got this human life; what can I do to get the most out of it?" And the answer should be, "I'm going to do the best I can to find true happiness, something dependable, something to show for all the suffering I've been through as I take birth, age, grow ill, and die."

So we should think about these issues as we meditate. We're not getting into the present moment just to stop there. That would be like someone who, after wading through a dense jungle, finally gets to a road—and then lies down on the road, forgetting that the road is there to be followed to see where it leads you. When you get into the present moment, that's not enough. You have to learn how to ask yourself the right questions about the present moment, in particular, "What are your intentions right now, and what results do they have? Where are they going to take you?"

Intentions just don't float in and out of the mind without leaving a trace. They leave their mark. They do have results. Are you satisfied with the results? If not, what can you do to get better results? Learning how to ask these questions, the Buddha said, is what gives rise to discernment so that your actions go beyond just the ordinary, mundane level. As he pointed out, there are four kinds of action: actions that are skillful on a mundane level, actions that are not skillful on the mundane level, actions that are mixed, and then actions that take you beyond the mundane level, that open you up to the Deathless and bring you to the end of action. That fourth kind of action is what he says is really worthwhile. That's what's special about his teaching. That's what's distinctive about his teaching. He discovered that the principles of causality work in such a way that you can bring yourself to the Uncaused by being as skillful as possible in what you do. And the discernment that shows you how to act in those ways, that detects what in your intentions is skillful and what's unskillful, what in the results of your actions are satisfactory or not: That's what guides you in the right direction.

You take your desire for happiness, and you take it seriously. It's not that the Buddha condemns all craving. There's a passage where he says, "There is a kind of craving that has good results—the craving that leads you away from repeatedly wandering on, the desire to get out of this wandering, to discontinue this wandering." So you take that desire—which is what the expression of *metta* is all about, the desire for happiness, both for yourself and other people—and you add to it the conviction that you can do things that lead to happiness. You take that desire, you take that conviction, you put them together with a good dash of heedfulness, and then you try to watch as skillfully as you can to see what you're doing. Monitor the results of your practice and adjust them as necessary. These factors all taken together are the recipe for the discernment that leads to release.

There's no one technique that can guarantee that you'll gain discernment, just as there's no one technique that has a monopoly on giving rise to discernment. The techniques are things that you use in your quest for discernment, but your quest has to be informed by more than techniques. It has to be informed by the right questions, by the right qualities of mind, by the rigor you bring to your attention to what you're doing, by your willingness to set the highest possible standards for yourself, your unwillingness to settle for a happiness that falls under the three characteristics.

That's how liberating discernment comes about.

Producing Experience

November 12, 2002

A friend of mine once wrote a novel about a storytelling contest among the gods of the Taoist heaven. In the course of the novel you read about the gods conducting their story contest—it's the male gods lined up against the female gods, but there are traitors on both sides—and you also read the story they invent, alternating from one side to the next. The story's full of all kinds of suffering: A young woman gets sold as a slave to get her parents out of debt; her new master is a good person, but he dies off pretty quickly; he's got an evil brother, and all kinds of horrible things happen; there are floods, fires, suicides, lots of injustice—what makes for a great story but a miserable life. And then at the very end of the novel Kuan Yin appears and tells the Taoist gods, "Well, now that you've told this story, you're going to have to go down there and *live* it." The last image in the novel is of the Taoist gods all tumbling out of heaven down to the earth they've despised so much below. Of course, Kuan Yin here represents what Buddhism did to China: It brought in the teaching on kamma.

We're creating our lives. And even when the mind seems to be simply spinning its wheels, it's not just idly spinning its wheels. It's creating new states of being, new possibilities—some of which are good, some of which are not so good. You have to keep that principle always in mind as you're meditating. You're not simply here innocently watching what's going on without any responsibility for what you're experiencing. *You're responsible for your experiences—* through your actions in the past and in the present moment. On the one hand, this sounds a little onerous because nobody likes to take responsibility. On the other hand, though, it's empowering. If you don't like the present moment, you can create a new present moment because the opportunities to do so are endless.

We're not just consumers of experiences. We're also producers. We have to keep this principle in mind as we go through the practice. Our training in the precepts reminds us that we shape our life by the choices we make in what we say and do. Our training in concentration teaches us that how we approach the present moment is going to make a big difference in how the moment is experienced. You can develop skill in the way you focus on the breath, the way you adjust the breath, the way you develop sensitivity to what's going on in the body. These are all things you do as a producer of experiences, and you can learn to do them more and more skillfully to create a sense of wellbeing in the present moment.

Even when there's pain in the body, even when there are other difficult issues in life, you can create a still center for yourself. You don't have to be a victim of what comes in from outside. You don't have to be a victim of whatever comes welling up from within the mind. You have a role right here, right now, in shaping things, and— as you develop more mindfulness, develop more alertness, as your powers of concentration get more and more solid—you have the tools you need to make that present experience a lot more livable.

The same principle holds true as we try to develop discernment. We're often told that discernment consists of seeing things as inconstant; and because they're inconstant, they're stressful; and because they're stressful, they're not-self. Now, most of us in the West are used to consuming our experiences. We don't buy a Ford Explorer. We buy the Ford Explorer experience. We go to Yosemite for the Yosemite experience. If we take the Buddha's teachings on discernment out of context and put them in our normal consuming mode, what do they seem to say? They seem to say, "Life is short. Experiences are fleeting. Grab as much pleasure as you can." And since you can't hold onto things for too long before they change, you have to try to embrace them, appreciate them, squeeze as much as you can out of your experiences, and then be quick to let go before they start falling apart. But that's okay because other experiences will come along, so that you never run out of things to embrace. In other words the teaching seems to be telling us how to be expert connoisseurs in consuming our experiences.

Taking the teachings out of context leads to other misunderstandings as well. You begin to think, "If everything's impermanent, why spend all this time trying to develop concentration? It's all going to end someday anyhow. Why try to develop good qualities in the mind? They'll all come to nothing eventually. Why don't we just accept what we've got and learn to enjoy that?" But that's taking the teachings out of context.

When the Buddha taught the teachings of discernment, he started with questions of, "What's skillful? What's unskillful? What can I do that will lead to long-term happiness?" This is the first set of questions you're supposed to ask to develop discernment. If you look at your normal patterns of consumption, you begin to realize that a lot of them are very unskillful: They lead to only short-term types of happiness. And you realize it's not just the consumption, but it's also what you do to produce these experiences that's unskillful. You find yourself acting on greed, anger, passion, fear, just to get the experiences you want.

So to get out of that pattern you want to develop the skills that will make your happiness more solid, longer lasting, less likely to turn on you and eat you up. This is the type of discernment that underlies development in terms of virtue and concentration. You refrain from the activities that would lead to instant gratification but long-term regret, long-term remorse. You develop qualities of mind that create a sense of greater wellbeing that doesn't have to depend on outside stimuli, that can stand up against any kind of outside situation.

Once you've developed these qualities, you take the process of discernment a little bit deeper. Use that principle of inconstancy to ask, "Is there anything that's not inconstant? Do I have to keep on producing, producing, producing for the rest of eternity? Isn't there a type of happiness that doesn't require that?" So you turn and look more carefully at the type of happiness you're creating. Then you run into the question of, "Who's consuming this? What is this consumer? What is this producer?" You begin to see that the consumer is also made up of khandhas you've produced. And this insight makes the whole process seem even more futile. Why would you want to get involved in this process—creating experiences for experiences to enjoy? From this point of view, even long-term happiness isn't good enough. Your powers of sensitivity have been sharpened. Your insight into the process of production and consumption has gotten sharper as well. And when you finally reach the point where you see that it's not necessary, you let go.

If you were only a consumer, it'd be easy enough to continue enjoying things that are inconstant as long as you've learned to mind your manners in how you embrace things—hugging without grabbing—but as a producer there comes a point when you get tired of producing. You've had enough. You see that all the effort going into producing is simply not worth it. That's the insight that allows you to drop things, that allows you to let go.

And it's in that context that the teachings on the three characteristics have their true meaning, play their true role. Like the storytellers in the novel, we have to be careful about what we're creating because we're going to have to live in what we create. Keep asking yourself, "Is this good enough? Am I satisfied with what I'm creating?"—because it's not an easy task to stop creating. If it were easy, we wouldn't have to sit here and meditate so hard. It's difficult and, whether we like what we're creating or not, we keep on creating. That's the problem.

So as long as you're going to create, try to create as good a world for yourself as you can, as good a world for the people around you as you can, until you've developed the qualities where you can look into this world-production activity in your mind, this factory that keeps churning things out moment-by-moment-by-moment, to see if you can take it apart.

It sounds a little scary, but then the Buddha promises that once you take these things apart, there comes a happiness that nothing that you've created can ever compare to. This promise, together with the reality of that uncreated, unfabricated level of happiness: that's what makes all this work we're doing here more than worthwhile.

Mastering Causality

May, 2001

They tell us that the heart of the Buddha's Awakening was discovering the principle of causality, how cause and effect work to shape your experience. It sounds pretty abstract but it's actually directly related to what you're experiencing right now. In other words, there's the result of past kamma, there's your present kamma, and there's the result of present kamma. Those are the three things you're experiencing at any given moment.

Of course when we start out, it all tends to be mixed together. It's just experience. We don't see these patterns, we don't see the component factors as separate and distinct, so things seem pretty random. But if you learn how to look at what you're doing right now, you come to see that you're not totally passive. The things you're experiencing are not just coming in at you. There's an active side to the mind that goes out and shapes them, adds a little here, takes away a little bit there. You're getting sensitive to that aspect of the mind, to what you're doing right now. That's a large part of the insight you need to gain in the meditation.

Most of us are like a man who goes storming into a room, acting in an offensive way, and then later complains, "The people in the room seemed awfully defensive, awfully unfriendly"—as if he didn't have any impact on the atmosphere of the room through his actions, through the way he entered the room.

So how are you storming into the present moment? One way to find out is by checking on the breath. Exactly what are you doing with the breath right now? Is the breathing a totally passive, automatic process, or are you doing something to the breath? Is there some level of the mind that's making decisions? One way to find out is to make conscious decisions about the breath, nudging it a little bit here, a little bit there. We're not talking about making huge differences in the breath, just making gradual changes in whichever direction seems most comfortable.

As you do this you begin to realize that your present experience of pleasure or pain depends on decisions you're making right now. You begin to get more sensitive to what the mind is doing, particularly in terms of its perceptions and thought-fabrications, and how these relate to your feelings.

Perceptions are the labels you put on things. For example, you may experience the body as something solid breathing in and breathing out. Well, you can change that perception. See everything you sense in the body right now as an aspect of the breath property. Look at it that way: every sensation as a type of breath sensation. See what that does to your sensation of the body, the way you relate to it, the way you evaluate it, the way you breathe.

And then your thought-fabrications: Use them to ask questions. How about breathing this way? How about breathing that way? And so you give it a try.

As you do this, you get a greater and greater sense of how much you really are shaping your present experience. Then you can take this insight and apply it to issues of pain, both physical pain and mental pain. Most of us tend to think of ourselves as passive recipients, victims of a particular pain attacking us. There doesn't seem much we can do about it. That's because we have a habitual way of reacting to pain. Unless we can change that habit, we're not going to see much improvement in the issue of why we're suffering, of how we suffer.

But if you really look at a physical pain, you realize that while part of it comes from something wrong with the body, another part comes from what the mind is doing to manage the experience of pain: the way it paints a mental picture of the pain, the way it latches onto that mental picture, what it's doing to maintain the pain in a particular way or to move it in a particular direction. That's going on all the time, yet we're not really aware of how much we're contributing to our own pain. That's the big issue.

That's the first noble truth: the pain we're creating through our clinging, craving, and ignorance.

To see these things, you have to be very, very sensitive to the present moment and very sensitive to what your input is. This is why concentration is so important, getting the mind really still so that it can see these things very precisely. For instance, when pain arises we tend to miss the fact that the mind is constantly labeling it, "Pain, pain, pain, pain, pain." And in addition to the label of "pain" we sometimes paint a picture of it to ourselves. That act of labeling, if there's clinging along with it, contributes to the pain. And when you get really sensitive to the movements of the mind— and this requires getting the breath really still so that it's not interfering with what you're seeing—you see that there's a constant repetition going on in the mind. Sometimes the labeling, the clinging, and the repetition are so insistent that the physical cause of the pain has long since gone. The act of clinging is the actual pain you're experiencing now.

So when you learn how to see, "Oh, there's that mental label going again, there it goes again, there it goes again": Can you stop it? See what happens when you stop it, when you just drop it. You'll find that your experience of the pain changes. That's when you gain insight into the issue of what you're doing in the present moment, how you contribute to the shape of your experience.

That's a lot of the meditation right there—just sensitizing the mind to what it's doing. Most often that's our big blind spot: what we're doing right now. We're so conscious of what other people are doing—"They did this to me, they did that to me"—but we're not looking at what *we're* doing, which is why what they're doing causes us pain. Many times you can't avoid what's coming at you from the outside—it's past kamma—but you *can* avoid the unskillful ways you're reacting to it. Sometimes you find that the way you're reacting to the situation feeds back into the situation, influencing what those other people are doing and making the situation worse. But even when that's not the case, you find that your suffering really comes from the way you relate to the outside situation.

That's what the first noble truth is all about, clinging to the five aggregates: clinging to the form of the body, clinging to your feelings, perceptions, thought-fabrications, or consciousness. When you stop clinging to these aggregates, then even though they're still impermanent and there still may be some stress in them, it doesn't weigh on the mind. The bridge has been cut so that it doesn't connect. You stop lifting things up, as in Ajaan Suwat's image: The mountain may be heavy in and of itself, but if you're not trying to lift it up then it's not heavy for you.

So you've got to see where you're doing your heavy lifting and then try to understand why. Only when you understand *why* you're doing things can you really stop. Sometimes in the course of a meditation you can force yourself to stop, but if there's no real understanding, then as soon as the mind gets back to its old ways, it goes lifting things, picking them up, carrying them around again. But if you look into *why* you're lifting these things, what misunderstandings lie behind what you're doing, why you feel that you have to carry these things around: That's a lot of the insight right there.

It's an old habit, the way the mind contributes to things in the present moment, particularly the ways it causes itself unnecessary suffering. We think that an undercurrent suffering is a necessary part of experience, but it's not. When you see it as stress, when you see it as a burden and you realize that it's not necessary, that's when you really let go.

So check on exactly where you're clinging right now, where you're contributing to unnecessary suffering. Try to make the mind as still as possible and then stay there to observe: "Is there still some stress here? Is there still a sense of burdensomeness here? What else is going along with that? Can you see any activity, any intention that's going along with that stress?" And if you catch sight of that activity, that intention, you drop it.

It's almost invariably something you didn't realize you were doing, something you were holding onto, in the sense of repeating it mindlessly. Sometimes you're aware that you're holding onto the act of intention, but you think you've *got* to hold on: "This is the core of my being, this is who I am, this is the way my mind has to work." Well, it doesn't have to work that way. Learn how to question those assumptions. Learn how to let go a little bit. This loosens things up in the mind. The things you never saw before, now you suddenly see.

This burden you create for yourself is totally unnecessary. What you thought was necessary, the way things had to be: They don't have to be that way at all. That's the whole message of the Buddha's Awakening: the principle of causality we've been talking about. He applied it to see how the suffering the mind experiences in the present moment is not necessary. That's why the principle of causality was so important. He realized the input he was putting into the present moment that was creating the suffering and he learned to stop.

And what happened when there was no input in the present moment? As we meditate we find that our input gets more and more and more subtle. Oftentimes we're not even aware of any input. We tell ourselves that we're sitting here perfectly peaceful, perfectly calm, nothing's going on, but actually there's a lot going on in the mind that we're missing. It's in a blind spot. When you begin to see that blind spot, begin to let go of what's in there, that's when things open up, that's when the meditation can really start making a radical change in the mind. A lot of the relationships in your mind—where you thought, "This is that way and that's this way"—you begin to realize are not necessarily so. And the realization that they're not necessary: That's where the liberation lies.

So a continuity runs throughout the whole process of meditation from the very beginning. If, while you're sitting here, the mind slips off, just bring it right back. If it slips off again, just bring it right back again. Even this much can make you more conscious of what you're doing in the present moment. You get more conscious of how the mind has its blind spots and you learn to make them more and more and more subtle, less dominant in the mind. In other words, you try to cut through them as much as you can. What happens, of course, is that they find more subtle ways to hide, but at least you gain a measure of control over the mind and a greater sense of what you're doing in the present moment.

That's crucial to the meditation. You keep applying that principle to more subtle levels, for the same principle holds all the way through. It's just that as you keep working on it, it requires more precision. But that's something you can develop. After all, this is a skill. That's another one of the Buddha's great discoveries. The ability to learn the path to liberation is a skill you can master in the same way that you master other skills: looking at the results of your actions, reflecting back on what you did, and trying to adjust things so that they keep getting more and more precise, more and more subtle, less burdensome to the mind.

Awakening isn't something that just drops on people without their being aware of what they're doing. It's not an accident or something that comes from outside. It requires that you get really sensitive to this teaching on kamma: "I am the owner of my actions." You're acting right now, so be very careful about what you do, in the same way that you'd be very careful about building a fire, careful about sharpening a knife, careful about all the other skills you need in life. It's just that, in dealing with the mind, you need to be even more careful, even more precise. It requires more subtlety. But this simple process of just getting more skillful in how you relate to the present moment: That can take you all the way to Awakening.

And that right there is revolutionary.

The Six Properties

March, 2003

In English we have a very limited vocabulary for describing how the body feels from the inside. We feel "tingly" or we feel "heavy." We have ants crawling on our skin or butterflies in our stomachs. There are not that many words, and nothing really systematic. This is where the Buddha's teaching on the properties is helpful. It provides a systematic way of categorizing the feelings you have in the body—how the body feels from the inside—along with a sense of what you can do with those feelings. This teaching also gives you a very clear sense of how much your present input shapes the way you experience the body, and an immediate, very visceral way of using that present input to balance things out, to make the body an easier place in which to settle down.

The texts list the properties as six: earth, water, wind, fire, space, and consciousness. It sounds like medieval chemistry. We'd do better though, to look at these properties as ways of categorizing the sensations that make up the way the body feels from the inside. The *earth* sensations are feelings of heaviness or solidity; *water* would be cool sensations; *fire* is of course warm; *wind* is the motion back and forth; *space* is the feelings of emptiness; and *consciousness* is the property that's aware of all these things.

The theory behind these properties is that they get provoked. In other words, as they get emphasized, as some incident strengthens them or kicks them into action, they get stronger. On the external level, natural events occur when the external properties get provoked. Floods come from the provocation of the water property; huge fires or intense heat, from the provocation of the fire property; huge winds, from the provocation of the wind property. Interestingly, the texts also attribute earthquakes to the wind property. This means that wind refers not only to the wind in the air, but also to the motion down in the earth. Apparently earth was the only property that wasn't provokable, on the external level at least, but it would move when the wind property got into the act.

Whatever we may think of these concepts as ways of describing external events, they're a very useful way of looking at internal events, at the experience of the body as sensed from within. Classically, the internal properties are used to explain disease. Giddiness or lightheadedness is a sign of too much wind property, a sign that the wind property has been provoked. With fever, of course, the fire property has been provoked. A feeling of lethargy or heaviness in your limbs is a sign of too much earth property.

These are things you can play with in your meditation. That's where the teaching really becomes useful, because it allows you to see how the way you focus on the body has an impact on how you perceive the body, how you actually sense the body. We think of sensations as being primary, the raw material, the basic building blocks of experience, but there are conscious decisions being made that precede the sensations. Look at the teaching on dependent origination. *Sankhara,* or "fabrication" is way down there, prior to the sensations you feel in terms of form, feeling, and so forth.

So how are you going to fabricate the body? If there are feelings of tension in the body, sometimes that's a sign of too much earth property, so you can think of the breath. This is one of the reasons we start with the breath. It's the property that's most easily manipulated—classically it's called the *kaya-sankhara,* the factor that fashions the body. It's also the property that most directly works through tension. Wherever there's a sense of tension, focus on it and see if you can get a sense of gentle, healing motion going through it. The potential for motion is there, simply that the perception contributing to the tension has blocked it. So you can consciously decide that you're going to perceive motion there. Give it a chance to happen, and the potential for motion, the potential for movement through that part of the nervous system, will get strengthened, will get aroused—which may be a better way of translating the word that I just translated as "provoked." The breath-potential gets aroused. When your awareness of the breath is aroused or heightened, it can move through that sense of blockage.

When you're feeling giddy or manic, you can think of the earth property to settle things down. If there's just too much frenetic energy in the body, you can think of your bones being made of iron, of your hands and feet weighing a ton. Wherever you have a sense of solidity in the body, focus on that and try to magnify it. You find that your choice of the image you're using, your purpose in choosing it, will really affect the way you start sensing that part of the body. Then you can take that sensation and spread it out, connecting it with other sensations of solidity in the body. The potential for solidity is always there.

When you're feeling depressed and weighed down, think of lighter sensations, of the breath giving a lift to the different parts of the body. When you're hot, think of the water property. Focus on whatever sensations in the body are cooler than the others. Really keep your focus right there, and think "water, water" or "cool, cool." You'll find that other cool sensations in the body will appear to your awareness. The potential for them was waiting, simply that they needed the element of present intention to highlight them.

When you're feeling cold, focus in on warmth. There will be some part of the body that's warmer than the others, so focus in on it. Think of the warmth staying there and spreading to other parts of the body where other warm sensations will get aroused.

You can do this at any stage in the concentration, although it's most effective when the breath is still. At that point the body feels like a cloud of mist, little points of sensation, and each little sensation has the potential to be any one of these four properties. When your sense of the body is reduced to what the French would call pointillism, it's a lot easier, simply with a thought, to emphasize either the heaviness or the lightness, the movement, the warmth or the coolness of those sensations, the *sensation-potentials* you've got there. This way you accomplish two things at once. On the one hand you balance out the body. Whenever one type of sensation feels too oppressive, you can think of the opposing sensation to balance it out. On the other, you start seeing the role of present intention in your awareness, in your experience of the present moment in a very visceral way.

When things grow very still and balanced in terms of these four properties, with this mist of potential sensations that can go in any direction, you can also focus on the space between the points. Realize that the space is boundless. It goes through the body and out in all directions. Just think that: "infinite space." Stay with the sensation of infinite space that comes along with the perception. The potential for it is always there; it's simply that the perception arouses it. It's a very pleasant state to get in. Things seem a lot less solid, a lot less oppressive. You don't feel so trapped in the body.

Ajaan Fuang once had a student, an old woman, who started practicing meditation with him when he was getting ready to leave Wat Asokaram. After he left, she had to practice on her own for quite a while. One evening, when she was sitting in meditation with the group in the meditation hall, a voice came to her and said, "You're going to die tonight." She was a little taken aback, but then she reminded herself, "Well, if I'm going to die, the best way is to die meditating." So she just sat there and watched to see what would happen as the body dies, to see what it would be like. There was an actual sensation of the body beginning to fall apart. "All of the various properties were going their separate ways," she said, "like a house on fire. There was no place in the body where you could focus your awareness and have any sense of comfort at all." So for a moment she felt lost, but then she remembered, "Well, there's the space property." So she focused in on the space property, and all that sense of the house on fire suddenly disappeared. There was a very strong sense of infinite space. There was always the potential to go back to the body. (This is something you'll notice when you're at this point in your meditation: There are the spots that could provide a potential for the form of the body but you chose not to focus on them. Instead you focus on the sense of space in between and all around. There's a sense of boundlessness that goes with it.)

When she came out of meditation, of course, she hadn't died. She was still alive. But she had learned an important lesson, that when things get really bad in the body you can always go to space. Even though it's not Awakening, and it's not the unconditioned, still it's a lot better than being immersed in turmoil along with the properties in the body.

So the properties provide a useful way of looking at the potentials in the present moment. They also make it easier to get to that sense of *awareness itself* that you read about so much in the writings of the Thai Ajaans. Once you're with infinite space, drop the perception of "space" and see what's left. There will just be a perception of *knowing, knowing, knowing*, which takes its place. You don't have to ask, "Knowing what?" There's just *awareness, awareness,* or *knowing, knowing*.

Once you've got everything divided up into properties like this, you've got the raw materials for gaining insight. The terms of analysis may initially seem strange, but once you get a visceral sense of what they're referring to, you'll find them extremely useful. They not only give the mind a good place to settle down in the stillness of concentration, but they also help you gain insight into the way perception shapes your experience of the body, shapes your perception of what's going on here in the present moment, seeing how fabricated it all is. You've got potentials coming in from past kamma, but you've also got the element of present choice, which becomes extremely clear when you analyze things in this way.

When I first went to stay with Ajaan Fuang, he had me memorize Ajaan Lee's *Divine Mantra*: six passages dealing with the different properties. For a long time it seemed very foreign to me until one night I was chanting the passage on the property of consciousness and I realized that it was referring to the awareness that's right here. *This* awareness. *Right here.* When this realization hit, it was as if a huge iceberg in my heart suddenly melted. I wasn't dealing with some outside, foreign frame of thinking; instead, it was something extremely direct, immediate, right here and now. That was when I began to get a sense of why Ajaan Fuang had asked me to memorize the chant, why he wanted all of his students to think about their present experience in terms of the properties.

So keep this mode of analysis in mind. Try to get some sense of it as you put it to use, and you'll find that it's extremely useful in the practice. As with all of the Buddha's teachings, the importance of the teaching is what you do with it, and what it does for you in helping to gain insight into how stress and suffering are created in the present moment—and how you don't have to create them, if you pay attention, if you work at these skills.

Fabrication

March, 2001

The mind has a basic habit, which is to create things. In fact, when the Buddha describes causality, how experiences come about, he says that the power of creation or *sankhara*—the mental tendency to put things together—actually comes prior to our sensory experience. It's because the mind is active, actively putting things together, that it knows things.

The problem is that most of its actions, most of its creations, come out of ignorance, so the kind of knowledge that comes from those creations can be misleading. For this reason, what you want to do in the process of meditation is to back up, to get down as close to this process of creation as you can, to see if there's a way to do it skillfully that leads to knowledge, that leads you to a point that breaks through ignorance. And this means, instead of building up a lot of things, you let things fall apart so you can get down to exactly where these basic forces in the mind are putting things together.

Now it so happens that when we bring the mind to the breath, we have all these basic forces right here in their most elemental forms. The breath is the factor that fashions the body. It's what they call *kaya-sankhara* or the "physical putting-together." The breath is what puts life together in the body. If it weren't for the breath here, things would start falling apart really fast.

Then there's verbal fabrication, *vaci-sankhara*, the act of putting things in words. The two basic verbal sankharas are directed thought and evaluation. And you've got those right here, too. You direct your thoughts to the breath and then evaluate the breath: How does the breath feel? Does it feel good? If it does, stay with it. If it doesn't feel good, you can change it. This is about the most

basic level of conversation you can have with yourself. "Does this
feel good or not? Comfortable or not? Yes. No."

And then you work with that. What are you working with?
You're working with mental fabrication, *citta-sankhara,* which covers
feeling and perception: feelings of pleasure, pain, or neither pleasure
nor pain. And then perceptions are the labels the mind gives to
things: "This is pleasant. This is painful. This is this and that is that."

When you've got the mind with the breath, you've got all of
these things brought together: the feelings that come with the
breath, the perceptions that label the breath: "Now the breath is
coming in. Now the breath is going out. Now the mind is like this.
Now it's like that." The directed thought and the evaluation are
there as well, keeping you focused on the breath and on evaluating
the breath. So these things are all together. If you stray away from
here, you're usually straying away into distraction, into the realm of
further elaboration, in which you lose this basic frame of reference
and create a whole other one. It's what they call "becoming" in the
texts, when you create other worlds in the mind. Once you get into
those other worlds, you lose touch with the process of creation.
You lose touch with how becoming is brought together. So you've
got to learn how to take those worlds of distraction—and the
processes that form them—apart.

The Buddha talks about various ways of dealing with distraction. Once you've realized you've left your original frame of
reference, you bring yourself back. In other words, you remind
yourself. In some cases, the simple act of reminding is enough to
disperse that other little world you've created for yourself and
come back to this one.

Other times you have to reflect actively on the drawbacks of that
other world, of the thinking that creates it, especially if it's thinking
imbued with lust, aversion, delusion, or harmfulness. You've got to
remind yourself, "What would happen if I thought about this for a
while?" Well, you'd create certain habits in the mind, and once those
habits are imbedded in the mind they lead to actions that can create
all kinds of problems. When you see the drawbacks of that kind of

thinking, you say, "I don't need that. I've had enough of that in my life." You drop it and come back to the breath.

Other times you can consciously ignore the distraction. A little world appears in your mind and you say, "I don't want to enter into that," but for some reason it just doesn't go away. You realize the reason it's not going away is because you're paying attention to it. Even if you don't like it, paying attention to it is enough to keep it going—like a tar trap. You touch the tar with your hand and you get stuck. You try to pull yourself loose from the tar with the other hand and you get both hands stuck. Pull yourself off with your foot, your foot gets stuck. Bite the tar, your mouth gets stuck. So the only way to deal with it is to not touch it. In other words, don't pay attention to it. You know it's there, but you just don't give it any mind. After a while, from lack of attention, it'll die away.

A fourth way of pulling yourself back is to notice that when there's this process of creation, when there are these little worlds you create in your mind, an element of tension goes with them. Things would be a lot easier if you didn't create these worlds, if you'd just relax whatever physical and mental tension supports these things. So look for the tension. Once you can locate it, just relax it. When you relax the tension, the thought goes away.

A fifth way, when none of these other methods work, is to tell yourself, "Okay, I'm going to clench my teeth, press my tongue against the palate, and *I will not think* about that other thing." In other words, just through the force of your will you force it out of your mind. This is the method of last resort: the one that's the least precise and works only as long as your will power lasts. But sometimes it's the only thing that will clear the air. If we were to compare these various methods to tools, this would be the sledgehammer. It may be crude, but you need one in your arsenal for cases when scalpels and Exacto knives can't handle the job.

So when one of these other little worlds gets created in your mind, you use whichever of these methods work to let go of it and bring yourself back to the most basic levels of the process of creation: the breath, directed thought, evaluation, feelings, perceptions. Stay right on this level.

What do you do with them on this level? Well, you can create levels of concentration in the mind. Concentration is a kind of creation, but it's a creation that instead of obscuring the process of what's going on in the mind actually makes it clearer. You create, but without leaving these basic levels of your frame of reference. In other words, you put them to use in a new way. You put feelings to use in a new way. You learn how to create a feeling of pleasure from the breath so that the pleasure gets more and more intense, more and more solid. Just the act of sitting here breathing gets really refreshing. And if you stay with the feeling as a feeling, in and of itself, it doesn't pull you off into other mental worlds. You stay right here. It feels good right here.

So instead of feeding on the pleasure in an aimless way, you do it in a systematic way. That way you can keep the mind with a sense of pleasure, a sense of rapture, and it doesn't wander off. That's what the concentration is all about. As it strengthens the mind, it gives direction to the mind. It takes the desire for pleasure and puts it to good use. Once the mind feels comfortable in the present moment, it's not going to wander off anyplace else. It feels good right here. A lot more satisfaction comes from the sense of ease right here than from the little bits and pieces of satisfaction coming from the other worlds you can create with your mind.

Again, this is a process of creation, but it's a lot more skillful than normal. It keeps things on a basic level where you're in touch with the process. You don't lose sight of it. It's like the difference between sitting out in an audience watching a play and being behind the stage. Behind the stage, you see the actual play, but you also see what goes on behind it. In that way, you're a lot less likely to get carried away by the illusion of the play.

Now, of course, pain is going to come into your meditation as well. Sometimes it's out-and-out pain. Other times it's more subtle. And again, as with the pleasure, instead of thinking that you're on the receiving end of the pain, a victim of the pain, you start putting it to use. The pain is there for you to comprehend. That's what the Buddha said in his teachings on the four noble truths: The task with regard to pain is to comprehend it. Once the mind is solid enough and stable enough so as not to feel threatened by the pain, it can analyze the pain on whatever level it may be, searing pain or more subtle stress. As you comprehend the pain, you start finding that you understand the mind a lot better, too. All the little animals in the mind that tend to gather around pain: You begin to notice who they are, what they are, and you realize, "That's not me. It's just these thoughts that tend to cluster around pain." If you want to identify with them, you can, but they're going to turn your mind into a menagerie. They're going to create a lot of turmoil. And so you learn how to let them go.

Even when you're focused on the pleasant levels of concentration, you'll find that as you get more and more sensitive toward these various levels, a subtle element of stress accompanies each one of them. Once you identify where that stress is, you let it go. That takes you to a more subtle level of concentration. You stay there for a while. In the beginning, you don't notice the stress in the new level. It's like going into a bright room where your eyes haven't yet adjusted to the light. At first you see nothing but the dazzle. But if you stay there for long enough, your eyes begin to adjust and you begin to notice, "Oh, there are shapes, there are forms, there are things in this room that you can see."

It's the same as you go from one level of concentration to the next. Take the stress of directed thought and evaluation, for instance. Once the breath really feels full, really feels satisfying, you don't need to keep evaluating it. You don't have to keep reminding yourself to stay with it. You're just there, there, there, there, there with a basic perception. You let go of the directed thought and evaluation, and *Bong*—you come down to a much deeper level.

You go through this step by step. You realize what an important role perceptions play in this, the labels you put on things. You're constantly labeling the breath. When the breath is still so that you can drop that label, you begin to label the sense of space that's left, then the sense of knowing that's left as you drop the label for "space," then all the way up to the sphere of nothingness.

That's still called a perception attainment. It's based on the label that the mind puts on the experience that keeps you there.

So again, you're with these very basic, basic levels of creation in the mind. When you start taking them apart, that's when things really get interesting. Instead of building, building, building up, you're letting go, letting go, letting go, bit by bit by bit. And then, of course, you're getting attached to the new level you reach, but it's a good attachment. Otherwise, you'd go floating off to other worlds. This attachment here, at least, keeps you in the present moment where things can begin to open up. And instead of elaborating on it, you keep applying the teachings of the four noble truths and keep the questions basic: "Where is the stress here?"

This is especially important when you get to the level of infinitude of consciousness or the infinitude of space. On those levels it's easy to develop a sense that you've reached the ground of being from which all things come and to which all things return. If you're not careful, you can really start philosophizing on this theme, elaborating on it, getting into all kinds of abstractions about the relationship between the absolute and the relative, emanation—all sorts of big, buzz-word issues. But they're totally irrelevant to the real problem in the mind—that there's still stress here. If you're still stuck here, you haven't gone beyond, you haven't reached the Deathless.

You've got to keep asking that same old basic question: "Where is there stress here?" Look for it. See what you're doing that keeps the stress going, see that it's unnecessary, and then let go. Ultimately you open up to something totally unfabricated.

So instead of building things up that pull you away from the present, you start by building up states of concentration in the mind. These are types of fabrication, of course, but they're the type of fabrication that keeps you within this frame of reference: the very absolute present. They don't distract you into other levels where you lose touch with the basic building blocks in the process of fabrication.

This is a basic pattern throughout the Buddha's teachings: Before you let go of things, you first have to learn to do them skillfully, mindfully, with awareness. The doing, the mastering of the skill, is what enables you to know them. This brings us back to that basic principle we talked about earlier: We wouldn't know anything, there would be no awareness at all, if there weren't any *doing* in the mind. You have to learn how to do things more and more skillfully until finally you can get to a level where the mind becomes too sensitive to do anything. And at that point it opens up to a totally different kind of awareness.

So you make use of what you've got. The Buddha noticed that all things fabricated have an element of stress. But what are you going to do? How are you going to get to the unfabricated? You can't use the unfabricated as a tool because that would be fabricating it, and that's not its nature. You learn how to use the process of fabrication in a more skillful way. You divide things up into the four noble truths. There's stress, the origination of stress, the cessation of stress, and the path. The path is a process of taking things that are stressful—these perceptions, these feelings, these processes of creation—and using them in a skillful way. So you use fabrication to undo fabrication and then finally reach a point where everything opens up to the unfabricated.

It's an extremely skillful path, a skillful approach. It takes the raw materials that we've got around us all the time—the activities that we ordinarily use to create experience—and teaches us how to use them in a more skillful way. Getting down to basics. Keeping away from abstractions. Once there's an abstraction in the mind, there's a new level of being in there, a new frame of reference; it pulls you away from the present. A lot of self-delusion comes through abstraction. A lot of opportunity for lying to yourself comes through abstraction. So we keep things basic. We keep our nose to the ground. Just look at the basic things we have: physical, verbal, and mental fabrication. Learn how to put them to the proper use. Use them more and more skillfully. Get more and more in touch with the actual process of fabrication right here in the present moment. That's where things open up.

At the Door of the Cage

July 30, 2003

Our practice requires a lot of letting go. We prefer to think that it involves letting go of things that we don't like while allowing us to hold onto the things we do like, but actually it requires a lot more letting-go than that.

Several years back I was leading a day-long discussion on the four noble truths. When we got to the third noble truth, the cessation of suffering, the passages we were discussing contained descriptions of nibbana, and the general consensus in the group was that they didn't like the sound of it. It seemed too alien, too foreign to be really appealing. Then we got to the fourth noble truth and we started talking about right concentration. That sounded very appealing: rapture and pleasure permeating the entire body. Those were things you really could get your mind around. They sounded compelling. And that's the way it is with the practice: You have to develop the fourth noble truth, the path of practice, before you can appreciate the third. You have to hold onto right concentration before you can let go into the Deathless.

The Buddha's strategy in teaching us to let go is to give us better and better things to hold onto. For example, he gets you to hold onto states of good concentration. Then when you turn around and look at things that would normally incite your lust, your anger, your desire or passion, you realize that they're not worth it. You'd much rather hold onto the stillness, the state of satisfaction, the state of wellbeing that comes with your concentration. So you burn your bridges behind you and hold onto concentration as your only true happiness in life. Only then, when the Buddha has you cornered like that, does he have you think of the drawbacks not only of the things you've already left behind but also of the concentration you're holding to.

Only when you see the drawbacks of concentration can you realize that the only alternative is the Deathless. The only thing that would really appeal to you at that point is the Deathless. That's when the door opens.

As the texts say, the first stage in insight is to focus on the drawbacks of anything that's fabricated. The next stage is for the mind to incline to the Deathless. Normally the mind will not incline to the Deathless unless it feels that that's the only way out. Otherwise it's always going to find some other place to go, some other corner to hide in. So you need to remember that the teachings on, say, the three characteristics—inconstancy, stress, and not-self—are part of a course of training, and that the different teachings make sense only in particular stages of the training. Only when you're in the right stage for a particular teaching will it do its intended work.

Ordinarily, we'd like to leapfrog over the concentration to get to the discernment, because we're very busy people, after all. We've got a lot to do in our lives, so we want to get to the main point of this Buddhism thing and then go on to something else. But that's not how the practice works. You have to put your mind in particular states, you have to get attached to particular states, before the teachings can function in the way they're supposed to. If you think about the inconstancy, stress, and not-selfness of things you're not attached to, it doesn't really make an impact. Or if you tell yourself that everything is inconstant, stressful, and not-self before the mind has a safe place to settle down, those thoughts can be really unsettling and disorienting. Only when you're in a relatively stable place mentally, and ready to look for a way out from even the subtle instability there, will those thoughts provide the way out.

Years back I was flying on an airplane where they showed the movie, *Close Encounters of the Third Kind*. I didn't have the soundtrack to go by, but even without paying much attention I found the story pretty easy to figure out. The hero had a miserable family life, and so when the opportunity came to step onto that humongous flying saucer and go off who-knows-where, he was willing to go. Now, if he had had a happy family life, a satisfactory family life, he wouldn't have gone. He would have been happy to stay home, and the prospect of going off with these weird creatures from outer space would have been too daunting. But the fact that his life was so miserable made him willing to take the leap.

In that case the leap was pretty strange. And, fortunately the Buddha doesn't ask us to be miserable before we leap to nibbana, but he does recommend that we develop a sense of disenchant-ment—*nibbida*—and that we do it skillfully. He teaches us to get attached to more and more refined states of wellbeing in the mind, and to become disenchanted with everything else. It's like climbing a ladder. To climb up the rungs of the ladder, you already have to be holding onto a higher rung before you can let go of a lower one. Finally when you get to the top of the ladder, when there's nothing higher to hold onto, nowhere else to go: That's when you get off onto the roof or wherever you're headed. That's when you can totally let go. In the meantime you've got to hold on. The same principle holds true in the practice: You let go of lower attach-ments only when you've got something higher to hold onto.

So when you're practicing concentration don't be afraid of being attached to it. In fact, you *should* get attached here. That's part of the whole dynamic of the practice. Allow yourself to be attached to the breath, get to play with the breath, make the breath a really com-fortable, good place to stay. As the breath gets more refined, you find that the mind goes through more refined stages. The two help each other along. The greater the refinement of the mind, the more refined the breath, and vice versa, back and forth. And you find that your concentration does go through clearly discernable levels. But again, don't be afraid of getting attached to them. The whole point is to want to be there, to want to develop the mastery that allows you to bring the mind to those levels whenever you need them, and to stay centered in them as long as you like. This is why the Buddha—unlike a lot of modern teachers—never warned his students against getting attached to jhana. In fact, his instructions when he sent them off to meditate were always very clear: "Go do jhana." And he wanted them to master it.

Ajaan Fuang once said you have to be crazy about the meditation in order to be really good at it. In the course of the day, whatever spare minute you can find to keep your mind on the breath, you want your mind to head there, again and again. It's almost as if you were addicted to it. They say that when alcoholics go into a house, one of the first things they pick up on is where the alcohol is kept. They're very conscious of that. Their minds incline in that direction, so that without even thinking they can detect the signs. Well, you want to be a breath-a-holic. Wherever there's breath, you want your mind to head there. Of course, you find that it's everywhere if you're really interested, if you really want to pursue it.

Again, it doesn't matter that you're attached to it. There are ways of ultimately prying you loose from that attachment. In the meantime it's a good place to be attached: states of concentration, states of wellbeing in the mind that don't have to depend on circumstances outside. That's a lot better than being attached to the sights, sounds, smells, tastes, tactile sensations, and ideas we're normally attached to. So allow yourself to cling here.

It's like the cages where they put birds. If you happen to open the door while the bird is clinging to the door, the bird can get out. That's what these states of concentration are: They're doors to the Deathless. When we say that the Buddha has you cornered, he's got you cornered right here at the door. If you hang on here, you'll eventually be able to open the latch and you'll be free. But if you're not here, if you're over hanging on the walls, then it's very easy for the person opening the cage to keep you in. Clinging to the walls doesn't get you free.

In other words you might think that you'd like to put an end to all your suffering, but if you're not really in the right place, it's not a door. You keep banging your head against the walls of the cage. But if you learn to hold onto these states of concentration, the time will come when they turn into doors. You'll develop a sense of dispassion not only for ordinary pleasures, but also for the peace you gain from states of concentration. You'll begin to see that no matter how good you are at the concentration, there will always be change, inconstancy in that concentration. And the time will come when the mind is simply fed up with that. It's had enough. That's *nibbida,* disenchantment. You're no longer enchanted with the concentration. You use it, but it doesn't have the same pull it had before. You want something better. That's when the mind can really incline to the Deathless.

As I told the people in that discussion group, the third noble truth may not sound attractive now, but as you get into the fourth noble truth and develop these states of concentration, you realize that the third noble truth really is better. It may not sound better in words, but when you're disenchanted with the fourth noble truth, you see that the third truth is the only direction where true happiness lies. Ultimately the mind will lean there, will incline itself there, because it's in a position to appreciate it for what it is.

So if you want to know what the Buddha was talking about and see if it really is something better than what we're experiencing now, this is what you work at: these stages of concentration. Direct the mind to the breath, evaluating the breath, really coming to appreciate what it is to be settled down, really coming to appreciate the state of stillness, and not chasing after things that keep running away from you through your senses.

Come to appreciate the sense of stillness you can gain with the breath. When you appreciate this, you'll be in a position to appreciate things that are even better—so that when you incline to something better, you find that you're actually right at the door of the cage. You can fly.

Glossary

Ajaan (Thai): Teacher; mentor.

Arahant: A person who has abandoned all ten of the fetters that bind the mind to the cycle of rebirth, whose heart is free of mental defilement, and is thus not destined for future rebirth. An epithet for the Buddha and the highest level of his Noble Disciples. Sanskrit form: *arhat.*

Bhava: Literally, "becoming." Mental or physical worlds, created through craving and clinging, in which rebirth can happen—either mentally, as when entering a mental world or a dream world; or physically, as when rebirth follows the death of the body.

Buddho (Buddha): Awake; enlightened.

Dhamma: (1) Event; action. (2) A phenomenon in and of itself. (3) Mental quality. (4) Doctrine, teaching. (5) Nibbana (although there are passages in the Pali Canon describing nibbana as the abandoning of all dhammas). Sanskrit form: *dharma.*

Jhana: Mental absorption. A state of strong concentration focused on a single sensation or mental notion. Sanskrit for: *dhyana.*

Kamma: Intentional act. Sanskrit form: *karma.*

Khandha: Aggregate; heap; pile. The aggregates are the basic building blocks of describable experience, as well as the building blocks from which one's sense of "self" is constructed. There are five in all: physical form, feeling, perception, thought-fabrications, and consciousness. Sanskrit form: *skandha.*

Metta: Good will; kindness; benevolence; friendliness.

Nibbana: Literally, the "unbinding" of the mind from passion, aversion, and delusion, and from the entire round of death and rebirth. As this term also denotes the extinguishing of a fire, it carries connotations of stilling, cooling, and peace. Sanskrit form: *nirvana.*

Pali: The name of the earliest extant canon of the Buddha's teachings and, by extension, of the language in which it was composed.

Sangha: On the conventional level, this term denotes the communities of Buddhist monks and nuns. On the ideal level, it denotes those followers of the Buddha, lay or ordained, who have attained at least their first taste of the Deathless.

Sankhara: Fabrication; fashioning. The forces and factors that fashion things, the process of fashioning, and the fashioned things that result; all things conditioned, compounded, or concocted by nature, whether on the physical or the mental level. In some contexts this word is used as a blanket term for all five khandhas. As the fourth khandha, it refers specifically to the fashioning or forming of urges, thoughts, etc., within the mind.

Sankhata: Fabricated.

Sutta: Discourse. Sanskrit form: *sutra.*

Wat (Thai): Monastery.

Inquiries concerning this book
may be addressed to:

The Abbot
Metta Forest Monastery
PO Box 1409
Valley Center, CA 92082 USA